THE
Wisdom
OF

עומק
הפשט

Avos

MOSAICA PRESS

THE HUTMAN EDITION

THE
Wisdom
OF

עומק
הפשט

Avos

RABBI YISROEL MILLER

Published by Mosaica Press, Inc.
www.mosaicapress.com
info@mosaicapress.com

In loving memory of

Gail Hutman, a"h

Zahava Golda Leah bas R. Yaakov Auerbach, z"l

An asker of questions, a seeker of truth,
but most of all, a loving mother.

"The more counsel, the more understanding;
the more charity, the more peace."

Pirkei Avos 2:8

THE HUTMAN FAMILY

In loving memory of

Martin Silver, z"l

A lovely, kind man who supported and encouraged those in need.
Humble, considerate, and caring, he was an inspiration
to all that knew him.

"Say little, do much, and receive everyone
with a pleasant countenance."

Pirkei Avos 1:15

Rabbi Levi Langer
Rosh Kollel / Dean

ז' כסלו ה'תשפא
November 23, 2020

Rav Yisroel Miller shlit"a has asked me to write a michtav beracha for his new sefer on Avos, and indeed I am pleased to offer my blessing : may Rav Miller, and this sefer , be blessed from heaven and may Rav Miller continue to teach us for many years to come. But I have something else to say as well, and I want to say it to you, the reader who has picked up this book:

Read the book.

You need to read this book because it will make you think. No doubt you have recited Pirkei Avos in shul, and perhaps some of its teachings did seep through by osmosis. But Avos is the mussar sefer that our Sages canonized in the Mishna. Shouldn't it have lessons that we need to think about? And how will we discover what those lessons are?

This book will make you think. It will make you think about what the lessons of Avos are, and about how you can internalize them and make them a part of your life.

I have been privileged to know Rav Miller for many years, and I know he has put careful thought into every page of this book. But what he really wants, is for his writings to stimulate you to contemplate what lessons Pirkei Avos holds for you. And then you can give those ideas some more thought, and figure out how to implement them in your own life.

Rabbi Levi Langer

Table of Contents

Acknowledgments

Over the years, I was privileged to give a number of *shiurim* on *Pirkei Avos*, and gradually I developed an approach that I believe to be important (for reasons given in the Introduction that follows), and which I applied to most (but not all) of the Mishnayos in the first three *perakim* and part of the fourth. I kept no notes and had no intention of publishing, but a former congregant, Benny Hutman, encouraged me to make the *shiurim* available, and he and his wife Esther graciously agreed to sponsor their publication. May Hashem bless them with all the *berachos* bestowed on *gomlei chassadim* and *mezakei ha'rabim*.

In working on the manuscript, I have also added more material so that those who have heard the *shiurim* will find something new as well. My explanations are only suggestions, and there may be much better ones found elsewhere, but I do believe that almost all of them will provide food for thought.

Special thanks to Rabbi Binyomin Halpern, who volunteered to help with arranging for the manuscript to be printed—one more kindness added to all those he has done for me over the years.

May the *Chonen Ha'daas* help all of us to discover the wisdom *Avos* has to teach, and may we be *zocheh* to be guided by it for a life of true success and joy.

Yisroel Miller
Tammuz 5781

Introduction

WHERE IS THE WISDOM IN PIRKEI AVOS?

Question: I would expect that *Pirkei Avos*, chapters of Mishnah devoted to character development and spiritual growth, would surely be filled with wisdom and profound insight. I believe that must be true, but for the most part, I haven't found it.

Many of the Mishnayos seem to say things that are self-evident, e.g., "Be cautious in judgment, and raise up many disciples." Would anyone believe that we should *not* be cautious or that we should have *few* disciples? Other teachings we might not have known, such as, "Do not converse excessively with a woman," are important, but they don't seem to be especially profound or insightful.

In studying *Pirkei Avos*, some use the Mishnah as a mere starting point to speak about a related topic, e.g., discussing prayer, humility, or the World to Come when teaching a Mishnah that touches on those topics. Others who analyze each Mishnah will often focus on small points, like an apparently superfluous letter *hei* (meaning "the"), while ignoring the main idea.

What is the ideal method of studying *Pirkei Avos*, and how can I try to understand its wisdom?

Answer: In this *sefer*, we use a revolutionary *old* approach to studying *Pirkei Avos*. This includes trying to understand the true meaning of each Mishnah, and how it applies to us.

There are many *mefarshim* available with various insights that may speak to your soul. But even when we merely read *Pirkei Avos* on our

1

own, we can benefit greatly by approaching each Mishnah with the following four points in mind:

1. If what the Mishnah says seems self-evident ("*Peshita! Mai ka'mashma lan?*"), ask yourself how someone might conceivably disagree with the Mishnah to try to discover the Mishnah's *chiddush*, the new insight.

2. If there is no new insight, perhaps the Mishnah is saying more than its simple translation reveals. *Mefarshim* will help you here.

3. *Avos* has no Gemara to explain it, but there are comments on *Avos* called *Avos D'Rabi Nosson* (published in the back of the Gemara), as well as other comments scattered through the Talmud (*Bavli* and *Yerushalmi*), many of which have been collected and published.

4. When one Mishnah makes several points, they may revolve around a single theme, and the whole may be more than the sum of its parts.

Insights to be gained from this approach will be found in the pages that follow, G-d willing.

Chapter One

כל ישראל יש להם חלק לעולם הבא שנאמר ועמך כלם צדיקים
לעולם יירשו ארץ נצר מטעי מעשה ידי להתפאר.

*Kol Yisrael—All Israel has a share in the World to Come, as it
is said: "And your people all of them are righteous, forever will
they inherit the land; a branch of My planting, the work of My
hands in which to take pride." (Yeshayahu 60:21)*

This Mishnah is not part of *Masechta Avos* but is taken from
Sanhedrin, yet it is a centuries-old custom to recite it before
reading or studying each chapter. It is also customary to end
each chapter with "Rabbi Chananya ben Akashia..." from *Masechta
Makkos*, and it seems likely that the reasons for adding these two selec-
tions are similar.

Picture a sincere young man or woman who resolves to keep every
halachah as perfectly as possible, and with great effort by and large suc-
ceeds. Then we tell them, "Excellent! Now here is *Avos*, with well over
a hundred *more* obligations of ethical behavior and character development, each of which is a challenge in itself, and you don't really measure
up until you've mastered them as well."

It's enough to make idealists throw up their hands and give up
in despair.

And therefore, before beginning a chapter in *Avos*, we say, "All Israel
has a share in the World to Come," i.e., *already*. You've made it, you're in
the winner's circle; now see how much more you can do. Just as in high

school, where only the top students take on extra credit instead of the students who really need it, so too should we approach *Avos* with the confidence of setting out to reinforce the success we already have (see the comments on "Rabbi Chananya..." at the end of this chapter).

א. משה קבל תורה מסיני ומסרה ליהושע ויהושע לזקנים וזקנים לנביאים ונביאים מסרוה לאנשי כנסת הגדולה. הם אמרו שלשה דברים הוו מתונים בדין והעמידו תלמידים הרבה ועשו סיג לתורה.

Mishnah 1: Moshe kibel—Moshe received the Torah from Sinai and handed it down to Yehoshua, and Yehoshua to the Elders, and the Elders to the Prophets, and the Prophets handed it down to the men of the Great Assembly. They said three things...

It seems that the Mishnah is coming to teach us the chain of Torah transmission from Moshe Rabbeinu to the Men of the Great Assembly (the Sages and last of the Prophets, who rebuilt Jerusalem and the Holy Temple). But there are questions:

1. While Moshe, Yehoshua, the Elders, and the men of the Great Assembly were one generation each, the Prophets spanned hundreds of years! If a list of American presidents reads "Washington, Adams, Jefferson, a bunch of others, Obama, and Trump," would we not find that odd?

2. Wouldn't the logical place to teach the chain of transmission be at the very beginning of the Talmud, in *Masechta Berachos*? Why place it in *Avos*?

3. Moshe, Yehoshua, and some of the Great Assembly were prophets too. Isn't the "Prophets" as a category somewhat misleading?

We may find the answer by asking a fourth question: The Mishnah continues and states that "they said three things," as did many other of the Sages in *Avos*, each one focusing on matters of particular importance and mentioning them often. But isn't every mitzvah, halachah, and character trait important, and aren't we meant to take *all* the lessons in *Avos* to heart? Surely each Sage taught his disciples all these lessons and more. Why then did each one limit himself to stressing only two or three points?

The answer is: This Mishnah is not coming to teach the chain of Torah transmission (this answers question 2), and neither is it a list of the generations (this answers question 1). Instead, the Mishnah is teaching us that Moshe, Yehoshua, the Elders, the Prophets, and the Great Assembly are five distinct *eras*, each era marking a change in the spiritual state of the Jewish People.

- "Moshe received the Torah from Sinai"—The greatest of all teachers, the greatest student, and the only sage who could resolve all doubts by asking the Source of all. This happened only once in history.
- "Yehoshua"—Chazal compare Moshe Rabbeinu to the sun and Yehoshua to the moon. As historian Rav Shlomo Rottenberg put it: "What is the difference between them? The difference between day and night!" Even so, Yehoshua towered over his peers as the one universally accepted Torah leader.
- "Elders"—A group. From them on, there were conflicting views, with a resultant lack of clarity.
- "Prophets"—There had always been prophets, but as *Sefer Shmuel* tells us, until Shmuel's time, the prophet was called a *"ro'eh,"* one who sees what is hidden from others. *"Navi"* means a speaker (as in *"niv sefasayim"*), one sent by Hashem to point out to the king or the people that they are fooling themselves (*Toras Avraham*). There had been serious sins in the past, but for the nation (or its leadership) to follow a long-term *pattern* of walking down a path of evil and calling it good, that indicated a new level of spiritual decline—a decline that has been with us ever since—that Hashem's prophets tried to arrest. (This answers question 3.)
- "Men of the Great Assembly"—Why were they called "great"? I would have said because they rebuilt the Jewish nation and the Beis Hamikdash, and formulated the text of the main prayers and blessings, among other achievements.

The Gemara gives a very different reason, saying that Moshe Rabbeinu praised Hashem as *"Ha'gadol, Ha'gibor, V'Ha'nora* (Great, Mighty and Awesome), but the Prophets who witnessed the destruction of Jerusalem and the Beis Hamikdash asked, "Where is His might and awe?" and they omitted those praises. The Men of the Great Assembly taught that Divine might and awe nevertheless remain, and they therefore re-inserted those words when they composed the *Shemoneh Esreh.* And though the Prophets at the time of destruction surely understood this too, nevertheless, since Hashem is a G-d of truth, "they did not speak falsely to Him."

What does this mean? If the Prophets also knew these truths, why did they not say them? And if in spite of their truth it was somehow "speaking falsely" to say them, how could the Great Assembly re-insert them into the davening?

The answer is that there are two kinds of truths: truths that we know in our minds but do not feel, and truths that we also feel in our hearts.

For example, Torah-Jews fully believe that listening to gossip is harmful, and they also fully believe that being struck by an automobile is harmful. Yet if our Torah-Jew sees a car speeding at him as he crosses the street, he will sprint out of the way, but if the town gossip approaches, he is unlikely to sprint at all. He knows in his mind the danger of *lashon hara,* but the dangers of automobile accidents is a truth he also feels in his heart. Rav Avigdor Miller called this deeper understanding "true knowledge" or *daas.*

In the time of the First Beis Hamikdash, prayers were said from the heart without a formal text, and Jews did not say praises they did not feel. The Prophets who lived at the time of the destruction understood that Hashem's greatness was undiminished, but after witnessing the horrors of the destruction, they could no longer feel that truth fully, and they therefore omitted those words.

The Men of the Great Assembly, who included the last of the Prophets, recognized that if the old system of only praying what we feel continued, the time would come when we could not pray at all.

They therefore taught that from then on (till today, as the Mishnah mentions no subsequent era), we must say truthful words of *tefillah*, even if we don't feel them, both to train us in *emunah* and to avoid losing *tefillah* completely. They also formalized the basic text of the siddur for the same reason.

But why are these eras, and the decline of the generations that they signify, recorded at the beginning of *Avos*?

If someone asks "Which mitzvos should a Jew keep?" the correct answer is, of course, "All of them." But if someone new to mitzvah observance, or even someone returning to Yiddishkeit after years of non-observance asks you which mitzvos *he* should keep, then you cannot give him more than he can chew at one time. He must progress step-by-step, and you must guide him to take those mitzvah-steps that are most appropriate for him at that particular time.

The Gemara tells us that David reduced the 613 mitzvos to eleven (principles), Yeshayah (who came later) reduced them to six, Michah to three, and Chavakuk to one (*Makkos* 24a). As the generations declined, the Neviim and Chachamim tried to give us a "handle" with which to grasp the Torah. With the end of prophecy and the old flame of inspiration no longer burning, different Sages of the Mishnah chose different teachings to emphasize. If we are too weak to try to grasp the whole Torah at once, at least we can focus on two or three points to give us a small handhold. (This answers question 4.)

> *They said three things: Be cautious in judgment, raise up many disciples, and make a protective fence around the Torah.*

These teachings seem to be almost self-evident, and I don't believe any of us would question them. But that being so, why do we need a Mishnah to teach us what we already know?

So let's ask: Might there be some reason *not* to be cautious, *not* to raise up many disciples, and *not* to make protective fences? Once we ask the questions, answers are not hard to find.

> *We do not teach Torah except to a student who is proper [hagun] in his deeds...The Sages said that anyone who teaches*

> *a student who is not proper is like someone who throws a stone to Markolis [a form of idol-worship]. (Rambam, Mishnah Torah, Talmud Torah 4:1)*

We can seek to determine the precise definition of "a student who is proper in his deeds," but we know that in the time of the Mishnah, it included being *"tocho k'baro,"* that one's inside matched his outside. If a student was sincerely devoted to serving Hashem, but his public piety exceeded the piety he felt inside (and who today can say that theirs does not?), he was *not* admitted to Rabban Gamliel's yeshiva. The bar was later lowered somewhat, but in the days of the Prophets, it possibly had been even higher.

We can understand the warning against accepting students whose deeds are not proper. A man with Rabbinic ordination who is dishonest, immoral, rude, or arrogant lowers the honor of the Torah and can do all sorts of damage. When the Men of the Great Assembly encouraged an increase in the number of disciples at the cost of admitting some who were less worthy, it was an *innovation* required by the times. Prophecy was coming to an end, national independence was gone, and maintaining the old standards might have resulted in too few students to carry on. The new teaching was necessary, and it was certainly new—not self-evident at all.

"Make a protective fence around the Torah"—Safeguards and protective fences are of great benefit, but their *cost* is that they can detract from the spontaneous, voluntary outpouring of devotion.

In the days of the Prophets, prayers were not recited from a siddur; you said what was in your heart, which is surely a better way to pray. But with the loss of prophecy and a general diminishing of holy enthusiasm, how much would we pray today if we had no fixed prayers to recite? Our first week's Shabbos morning minyan might daven for five minutes, and subsequent weeks would have no minyan at all. The Gemara says that the fixed prayers were created by the Men of the Great Assembly. It was a necessary protective measure, though not ideal, and this Mishnah is teaching something new—that generational decline will require more safeguards in the future.

"Be cautious in judgment"—We do not need a Mishnah to tell us to be cautious and not foolhardy. Rather, it means to err on the side of caution and to avoid risks that in earlier times might have been encouraged.

A wealthy man will often invest part of his money in high-risk/high-yield stocks, while the poor man with a small retirement fund is usually advised to invest more cautiously. As much as the poor man needs more money, he cannot afford to risk catastrophe, so better to be safe than sorry.

In the same way, in the days of the First Beis Hamikdash, when we had Hashem's Divine presence, prophecy, and national independence, we could afford risk-taking. One example was Shlomo HaMelech marrying pagan princesses who converted to Judaism only half-heartedly, as part of his plan to bring the world to Hashem with himself as Mashiach son of David.

It was a high-risk/potentially high-yield investment, which failed disastrously, but the crippled nation survived. In the post-Temple, post-independence era, we can no longer risk such investments, and therefore "be cautious in judgment," even if such caution might keep us from bold decisions we might otherwise make. *How much* caution and how much risk are of course judgment calls that the leaders of every generation must make anew.

ב. שמעון הצדיק היה משירי כנסת הגדולה. הוא היה אומר על שלשה דברים העולם עומד על התורה ועל העבודה ועל גמילות חסדים.

Mishnah 2. Shimon HaTzaddik was among the remnants of the Great Assembly…[This either means that he was one of the last surviving members of the Assembly itself, or that he was one of their disciples.] He used to say: On three things the world stands—on the Torah, on the service of Hashem [avodah], and on acts of kindness.

Since *avodah* and acts of kindness are also part of the Torah, the word "Torah" in this Mishnah means Torah *study. Avodah* ("service") refers to the service in the Beis Hamikdash or to prayer, but in contrast to the "mitzvos between man and man" that are acts of kindness, *avodah* possibly refers to all mitzvah-acts between us and Hashem ("between man and G-d"), with service in the Beis Hamikdash being the supreme example.

The ArtScroll Siddur translates "the world *depends* on three things," but the word "stands" means that these three are like foundations for the entire structure, with the absence of any one of them likely leading to total collapse. It is noteworthy that after the sin of the golden calf, when Hashem offered to make Moshe the father of a new people, Chazal say that Moshe answered, "if a chair with three legs—the Patriarchs—will not stand, how will a chair with one leg do so?"

A one-legged chair can be raised up but will immediately fall. A two-legged chair can stand like a bicycle but will then topple over to the side. The third leg keeps it up. In the same way, each of the three components elevates us, but we must have all three for the spiritual structure to endure.

Why is this so?

Avodah (both narrowly and more broadly defined) is the sole purpose of life on earth (see Chapter 1 of *Mesillas Yesharim* and the opening chapters of *Derech Hashem* for details). But without Torah study, we cannot know the basic halachos of how to serve, and all the more so the fine points of the higher spiritual levels ("an ignorant man cannot be a *chassid*"). Without Torah study, we might err even in understanding fundamental principles of faith and end up serving a being who is not Hashem at all.

Avodah without Torah study cannot stand, and Torah study without *avodah* is an empty intellectual pastime. But even the two of them together can lead to self-centered arrogance: It is *my avodah*, *my* piety, service to *my* G-d (not yours but mine, like some object I own). For the chair to stand, it must also have the leg of acts of kindness, drawing me out of myself to help Hashem's beloved children of whom I am only one.

The world stands on three things—each one vital in itself, and each one vital to the existence of the other two.

Shimon HaTzaddik's teaching is true in every generation, but it would not be out of place to note that in his lifetime, Shimon HaTzaddik witnessed the end of prophecy and Alexander the Great's conquest of Persia, with its accompanying ascendance of Greek philosophical rationalism. With spiritual values no longer front and center in society, it became all the more important to remind us of the world's true foundations—a reminder just as necessary to have today.

ג. אנטיגנוס איש סוכו קבל משמעון הצדיק הוא היה אומר אל תהיו כעבדים המשמשין את הרב על מנת לקבל פרס אלא הוו כעבדים המשמשין את הרב שלא על מנת לקבל פרס ויהי מורא שמים עליכם.

Mishnah 3. Antignos of Socho received from Shimon HaTzaddik. He used to say: Do not be like servants who serve the master for the sake of receiving a reward, but be like servants who serve the master not for the sake of receiving a reward, and let the fear of Heaven be upon you.

When the Mishnah uses the word "received," it means that Antignos was Shimon HaTzaddik's disciple and the leading teacher of the next generation. "Do not be like servants…but be like servants…" seems verbose. Had it said only, *"Be* like servants who serve the master" etc., would we not know, "Do *not* be" etc.?

Apparently, this is teaching two distinct lessons, possibly the following:

1. "Do not be like servants who serve the master for the sake of receiving a reward" who cease to serve if reward is not given, i.e., do not make your *avodas Hashem* contingent on your receiving blessing in *this* world. Eternal reward will surely be given in time, but that time is in the World to Come.

2. "Be like servants who serve the master not for the sake of receiving a reward" is teaching us the appropriate motivation for serving. Serving to receive reward in the World to Come is acceptable, but not ideal. If so, how *should* we strive to serve?

Some explain that the ideal service referred to here is to serve out of love, like servants who love their master. The difficulty with this explanation is that the word *"avadim"* in the Mishnah is more precisely translated as "slaves," and one must wonder how many slaves actually served their masters out of love. In addition, serving Hashem out of love is surely one of the greatest and most difficult spiritual achievements, yet Antignos is teaching this as if it were practical for everyone here and now.

Let us suggest that "servants/slaves who serve the master not for the sake of receiving a reward" are motivated not by love (which is rare) but by *loyalty*.

In Southern states during the American Civil War and even afterwards, there were slaves who stayed with elderly masters or with widows and young children out of compassion and a sense of loyalty, and readers of Sherlock Holmes stories know of the English house servants who stayed with one family for generations.

The importance of "family honor" and "upholding your family name" has been largely lost today, but old-time Jews (and even non-Jews) acknowledged that we are all part of a generational chain, and they felt the responsibility to be loyal to the faith of their fathers and to their fathers' G-d. We may not always feel enthusiasm, but that loyalty and sense of responsibility can keep us going, even with no thought of reward.

When I lived in Pittsburgh, our shul *gabbai* told me: "My father, may he rest in peace, used to open up the shul every morning for the 6:00 a.m. minyan. When he was in the hospital, he gave me his keys and asked me to open instead of him so that the men would not be kept waiting for *Shacharis*. My father never came out of the hospital, but I opened up the shul the next morning as he asked, and I've continued doing it every weekday for the last twenty years."

"And let the fear of Heaven be upon you"—To be loyal to Hashem is admirable, and to love Hashem is sublime, but even loyalty and love are missing an essential component of our relationship with Him—recognizing that He is the Lord, G-d, our King.

I love my dear friends and am loyal to them, but if I treat my father like my friends, I dishonor him and demonstrate my ignorance of what it means to be a son to a father. "Fear of Heaven," whether fear of Divine punishment or the fear that is awe (*yiras ha'romemus*), acknowledges that Hashem is King and I am His subject, a foundation upon which all else in the relationship is built.

ד. יוסי בן יועזר איש צרדה ויוסי בן יוחנן איש ירושלים קבלו מהם. יוסי בן יועזר איש צרדה אומר יהי ביתך בית ועד לחכמים והוי מתאבק בעפר רגליהם והוי שותה בצמא את דבריהם.

Mishnah 4. Yosi ben Yoezer of Tzeredah and Yosi ben Yochanan of Jerusalem received from them…

"From them"—Although Antignos was the leader of his generation, he was joined by hundreds or thousands of other Sages and teachers, and their successors studied and received the tradition from many of them.

"Yosi and Yosi"—Shimon HaTzaddik, and after him Antignos, occupied the position of Av Beis Din, leader of the Sanhedrin and highest Torah authority of the nation. Under the rule of the Persian and then the Greek kings, the Jewish political leader recognized by the rulers was the Kohen Gadol (High Priest), who was responsible for collecting taxes to pass on to the king. When the Kohen Gadol's incompetence resulted in unscrupulous men seizing power, the Sanhedrin created the office of the Nasi, a political leader who would deal directly with the gentile government. Yosi ben Yoezer was the first Nasi, with Yosi ben Yochanan serving as Av Beis Din, and the "*Zugos*," the pairs of Sages mentioned in the following Mishnayos, continued this tradition.

The Sanhedrin chose the Nasi from among the leading Sages, and as the nation's political leader, the Nasi was honored like a king. When Rome took over the country, they began selling the office of Kohen Gadol to the highest bidder, and there was great concern that they might do the same to the office of the Nasi. To prevent this, the Sanhedrin decreed that the office of Nasi (held at the time by Hillel) would from then on pass from father to son. Some of Hillel's descendants were great *talmidei chachamim* (e.g., Rabbi Yehudah HaNasi, editor of the Mishnah), but inevitably some were not, and after Rabbi Yehudah Nesiah (grandson of Rabbi Yehudah HaNasi), we do not find a Nasi involved in Talmudic discussions. The office itself continued until it was abolished by the Romans in the sixth century CE.

> *Yosi ben Yoezer of Tzeredah says: Let your home be a meeting-house for the Sages, and place yourself in the dust at their feet, and drink their words with thirst.*

"Let your home be a meeting-place for the Sages"—Even if you spend many hours in Torah study at the yeshiva or *beis ha'midrash*, even learning from and interacting with a *rebbi*, you should also try to get *talmidei chachamim* to spend time in your own home. Their presence creates a unique atmosphere, and even in their absence you see your rooms and furniture associated with their memory. Over the years, my wife and I have been privileged to have distinguished *talmidei chachamim* at our forty-year-old scratched and dented dinner table. The table and its history enhances the spiritual quality of our lives, and we have no desire at all to exchange it for a newer one.

"Let your home be a meeting-place for the Sages" surely means "have Sages meet in your home," but the wording seems also to be telling us to make our homes into suitable meeting-places, i.e., that our homes should be places in which the Sages would feel comfortable. Is the nature of the reading-material or electronic entertainment scattered around the house appropriate? Are our furnishings too lavish or ostentatious? And is there anything we would want to hide before the Sages arrive? There is perhaps no one answer suited to everyone, but surely everyone can make time to ask the questions.

"And place yourself in the dust at their feet"—A guest naturally feels beholden to his host, and it is natural for a magnanimous host to feel at least equal (if not superior) to the guest who is the object of his hospitality. The Mishnah warns us that serving as host to the Sages should not detract from the humility we need in order to learn. A chassid listening to words of Torah from his *rebbi* hears more (and remembers far more) than another student because reverence rivets his attention. A Midrash tells us to listen to any Torah speaker as if hearing Moshe Rabbeinu, which of course does not mean to refrain from raising challenges when warranted, but the attitude with which we initially pay attention makes a huge difference in how much we understand.

"And drink their words with thirst"—We pray that Torah study be enjoyable, but "thirst" indicates a sense of *need*. At a medical school class on stuttering, the student who knows he will soon be called upon to do the procedure listens far more intently than an outsider, because the student *has* to know how to do this.

I have never been interested in reading the manuals for automobiles I've owned, but after buying one particular car, I parked it that first evening and found myself unable to turn off the car's headlights. With visions of the battery draining, I reached for the glove compartment, clutched at the car manual, and read it carefully and thoroughly because I *had* to know the answer. So too with Torah. To feel a thirst, i.e., that I *must* have this information, is a major key to success in learning.

ה. יוסי בן יוחנן איש ירושלים אומר יהי ביתך פתוח לרוחה
ויהיו עניים בני ביתך ואל תרבה שיחה עם האשה. באשתו אמרו
קל וחמר באשת חברו. מכאן אמרו חכמים כל המרבה שיחה עם
האשה גורם רעה לעצמו ובוטל מדברי תורה וסופו יורש גיהנם.

Mishnah 5. Yosi ben Yochanan of Jerusalem says: Let your home be open wide, and the poor be members of your household, and do not converse excessively with a woman. In regard to one's own wife they said this; all the more so in regard to his neighbor's wife.

"Let your home be open wide"—Having lived in different communities, I have known many good people willing to offer hospitality to those in need. But I have also known a few very special people who were "the address" for *hachnasas orchim* (hospitality), the first name that came to mind and the last to ever refuse a request. That second group are those whose homes are "open wide."

"And the poor be members of your household"—Our father Avraham was the paragon of *chessed* (acts of kindness), not only in the deeds he did but also in how he did them. When travelers came into view, "he ran to them...and bowed: 'My Lords, if I have found favor in your eyes, please do not pass away from your servant.'"

It is uncomfortable to take charity, but Avraham made guests feel that they were doing *him* a favor by honoring him with their company. Even his nephew Lot learned this from him, bowing to travelers and begging them to stay with "their servant."

This is the meaning of our Mishnah's second statement: A "home open wide" is a great kindness to the needy, and making them comfortable by treating them like family ("members of your household") is kindness to their souls.

In regard to one's own wife they said this; all the more so in regard to his neighbor's wife.

The obvious connection between the beginning of the Mishnah and its end is that even when doing *chessed* and treating those in need like family, the boundaries of *tz'niyus* (modesty) must be carefully preserved. If the line is not carefully drawn, it is all too easy to cross it.

Two questions:

1. Why should it be wrong to "converse excessively with one's own wife"? (It should be pointed out that speaking to one's wife for any worthwhile purpose, including making her feel loved and appreciated, is not called "conversing excessively".) Some suggest that it refers to when the wife is in a state of *niddah*, but the Mishnah makes no such distinction.

2. "All the more so in regard to his neighbor's wife" implies that the danger in idle talk with another man's wife is *similar* to the danger of such talk with one's own wife, only greater. But the danger of closeness to another man's wife is of a different nature entirely! It seems that there is a specific reason to avoid "conversing excessively" with one's own wife—a reason we have not yet discovered—and that *same* reason applies to another man's wife, but with more force. What might that reason be?

Fortunately, the Sages themselves gave the reason in *Avos D'Rabi Nosson* (Chapter 7):

"If a man came to the *beis ha'midrash* and they did not treat him respectfully, or if he argued with his friend, he should not go and tell his wife...because he dishonors himself and his friend, and his wife who used to treat him respectfully now stands and mocks him."

"Honey, I asked for a raise, but the boss just called me a loser!"

"Dear, how terrible! How dare they treat you that way!" (But in her heart, she thinks, "I married a loser!")

So, the Mishnah is warning against conversing excessively with one's own wife because it may cause her to lose respect for him. But if that is the reason, what is the *kal va'chomer*, "all the more so with his neighbor's wife"? If your neighbor's wife has less admiration for you, that might be a good thing, not cause for concern!

But the Mishnah means to tell us that when men and women converse, it is always likely that there will be misunderstanding.

Conversation in general is much more than a straightforward exchange of information. Word choice, volume, tone of voice, facial expression, and eye contact convey a wealth of meaning that add to, modify, or even contradict the spoken sentences. Conversation between men and women is all the more difficult, because men and women use language and process information in very different ways. (There was a best-selling book on this subject, which I never read, but its title was something like: *Men Are from Mars, Women Are from Borough Park*.)

Add to the above the emotional static injected into any meeting between a man and a woman, one of whom might feel attracted to the other—whether consciously or not—and every conversation between men and women is a minefield waiting to explode.

Avos D'Rabi Nosson illustrates this idea with the example of a man who tells his wife how his friends treat him with disrespect. He thinks he is merely sharing information about his day and hopes for some sympathy. But he does not understand that his wife wants a husband she can look up to, and that she sees his social status as reflecting on her, and the news only causes her to lose respect for him.

Avos D'Rabi Nosson uses this case as just one example: If husband and wife, who understand each other as well as any two people can, and between whom there is no problem or emotional static of forbidden attraction, if even *their* casual conversation can ignite unexpected explosions, then *kal va'chomer*, how much more must one beware the unseen pitfalls of conversations with his neighbor's wife, when so much lurks beneath the surface of mere words.

ו. יהושע בן פרחיה ונתאי הארבלי קבלו מהם יהושע בן פרחיה
אומר עשה לך רב וקנה לך חבר והוי דן את כל האדם לכף זכות.

Mishnah 6. Yehoshua ben Perachiah and Nittai of Arbel received from them. Yehoshua ben Perachiah says: Make for yourself a rav, and acquire for yourself a friend, and judge every person in the scale of merit [dan l'kaf zechus].

"Make for yourself a *rav*"—Our *mesorah* (Torah tradition) places great weight on the importance of having a *rebbi*, and yet very many *frum* Jews, including alumni of major yeshivos, do not have one. Some had a *rebbi* but lost contact with him over the years, others had a *rebbi* who passed away, and others learned in the large yeshivos where becoming close to a *rebbi* seemed impossible. Whatever the reason, and no matter how valid the excuse, Yehoshua ben Perachiah is telling us to find a *talmid chacham* and make him yours.

Someone who was close to a great *talmid chacham* from the past generation may feel there is no one available today of the same caliber. Even so, "Make for yourself," choose from the best available and find ways to get close to him. Attend his *shiurim*, ask him questions, and if need be, make up questions to ask just to have an excuse to speak with him (*talmidim* used to do this with Rav Moshe Feinstein and Rav Yaakov Kamenetsky all the time).

Why is this so important?

1. Later in this chapter, it says, "Make for yourself a *rav* and avoid uncertainty (Mishnah 17)." We'll discuss this when we explain that Mishnah.

2. Chazal say that while Shlomo HaMelech's *rebbi* lived, Shlomo did not marry the daughter of Pharaoh. Shlomo surely thought his marriage was the right thing to do, but a fear of being put to shame by his *rebbi's* disapproval would have made him think twice or would have prompted him to ask his *rebbi* before doing it. Chazal even mourned the passing of a great colleague as the loss of *"gavra d'mistefina minei*—A man of whom I was afraid," whose challenges would force me to rule with extra care, and all the more so a *rebbi*.

3. A *rebbi* is also a source of invaluable help in decision-making. When I have presented a question to my own *rebbeim*, it is rare for them to simply tell me what to do. Instead, they would ask me what *I* believed were the relevant factors—pros and cons. With their Torah wisdom, their years of experience, and their knowing me personally, they would explain which factors were most important and why, and suggest a point or two I had not thought of. This often helped me reach a conclusion on my own, or if not, the advice they offered was almost always worth taking.

4. If at all possible, a married couple wants to have a *rav* who knows them both to help them with major decisions and *shalom bayis* issues, including giving a stern talking-to (to one or both) when appropriate. This relationship with a *rav* must be made long before issues come up, so that a long-established bond of trust becomes a resource available when needed.

"Acquire for yourself a friend"—Note that "friend" is singular. In the age of Facebook, some people have hundreds of "friends" but not one real friend; to have even one is precious.

A *"chaver"* is someone with whom you feel comfortable sharing fears and failures; someone who cares enough about you to tell you truths you don't want to hear, but to whom you are willing to listen because you know he truly cares; and who encourages you with admiration for your good qualities, even though he (and you) know about the other qualities that are not so good.

"Acquire"—Not with money, but by investing time and patience to put up with your friend's imperfections or ideas with which you disagree. If you and your friend don't often see each other, you'll have to make efforts through telephone calls and occasional visits to keep your friendship in good repair. Women seem to do better at this, but men need it just as much.

"And judge every person in the scale of merit"—To be *dan l'kaf zechus*, judging the other person favorably and giving them the benefit of the doubt, is a mitzvah in the Torah. But we know that this mitzvah applies only to judging mitzvah-observant Jews, yet the Mishnah says "every person," apparently including even non-Jews. And if we explain the Mishnah as referring only to judging observant Jews (which seems somewhat forced), why do I need a Mishnah to tell me to keep a mitzvah in the Torah?

Perhaps it means: Although the mitzvah applies only to judging observant Jews (and for some classes of wicked people, it is a mitzvah *not* to judge favorably), the Mishnah nevertheless advises us to make a habit of judging almost everyone favorably, for several reasons:

1. It makes us happier. There are many people who consistently think the worst of others, and they live lives of misery.

2. Rav Avigdor Miller said that someone who does not judge favorably will inevitably find himself disappointed by something their *rebbi* and their friend does, and will end up losing both.

3. "*Gam zu le'tovah*" and "all that Hashem does is for the best" is the act of judging *the Creator* favorably when something happens to upset us. If we are not in the habit of giving friends the benefit of the doubt, we are not likely to do so with Hashem either.

4. The experience of judging others favorably will give us a new insight; this is not so much an act of piety as it is one of *wisdom*.

We tend to think that being *dan l'kaf zechus* requires us to close the mind and open the heart. "I know what you did was terrible, but I am supposed to forget what I know and give you the benefit of the doubt, highly unlikely as it is." But so often when the facts appear clear to us beyond any doubt, we eventually discover that we were completely in error, often because of additional facts of which we were unaware.

Since I write this for my friends, including those friends I have not yet had the pleasure to meet, let me share two anecdotes in which I was involved:

I used to live in Pittsburgh on Waldron Street, a street that was only one block long. A Jewish young man on the block was jailed for selling drugs, and he bitterly complained to the Chabad chaplain that "Rabbi Miller called the police on me."

"Rabbi Miller, really?"

"Yes, he lives on my block across the street, and he called the cops."

The chaplain was surprised, and he contacted me about it. I explained to him that if the relatively small Jewish community like Pittsburgh had a second Rabbi Miller, the chaplain should surely know about it; but as it happened, there *was* a second Rabbi Miller, a retired Conservative clergyman, who just happened to live (of all places) a few houses up the block from me, who had apparently called the police.

(I'm not taking sides on the question whether the call was justified, only on how easy we can err even when we *think* we have all the facts.)

A second anecdote: I used to certify the *kashrus* of a local pizza shop. When the owner was absent, the counterman was in charge, a position held by a succession of workers.

One day, the owner was informed by the counterman that a stranger, by his appearance an Orthodox Jewish man, had come to the shop, gone to the basement as if checking the stock, and had then come up and ordered a pizza. When I heard about it, I was puzzled. It seemed rude for a stranger to inspect the stockroom, and if he had questions, my certification letter with my telephone number was prominently posted. When it happened a second time, I was more than a little peeved at his chutzpah. *If he doesn't trust my kashrus, why doesn't he go elsewhere,* I thought.

Eventually, the stranger's identity was revealed: Because of the turnover in employees, it sometimes took a few weeks before the new countermen got to know me. The impudent stranger checking the stockroom, with whom I had gotten so upset, was—me!

So, when it is so clear to me that the other fellow is in the wrong, I sometimes have the good sense to remember: I may not have all the facts, and even the facts I do have may mean something very different from what my poor brain believes right now.

ז. נתאי הארבלי אומר הרחק משכן רע ואל תתחבר לרשע ואל
תתיאש מן הפורענות.

Mishnah 7. Nittai of Arbel says: distance yourself from a bad neighbor, and do not associate with a wicked person, and do not despair of retribution.

"Distance yourself from a bad neighbor"—It would seem logical that my neighbor's bad behavior should not influence me to compromise my own, but logic as a determinant of human behavior is highly overrated. Even in a Torah community, there is pressure to have luxuries that others have and spend more than we can afford on *simchahs*. Advertising (even in *frum* periodicals) "kosherize" the lust for expensive clothes, vacations, and every imaginable kind of gourmet food (even proudly using the adjective *decadent*, which actually means "characterizing a state of moral decline"); and even the ads for Jerusalem apartments focus on upscale materialism instead of *kedushah*.

Non-Jewish attitudes also impact even mitzvah-observant Jews. The father who abandons his wife and children because "I owe it to myself to be happy," or the man who stops doing mitzvos with never a thought about *din v'cheshbon*, are just two examples of the many destructive attitudes that have crept in. This does not necessarily mean that we should cut ourselves off from the outside world entirely (nor is it possible), but at the very least it demands that we be aware of the dangers and do what we can to minimize them.

"Do not associate with a wicked person"—"even for purposes of a mitzvah," Chazal say.

The Chazon Ish was asked about this: If we join together with secularists in a mitzvah project, will not this association help to be *mekarev* them? Perhaps he might have answered that the possible benefit does not outweigh the harm. But it is reported that he said: "It is more likely to go the other way, because secular Jews are more sincere in their secularism than religious Jews are in their religiosity."

"And do not despair of retribution"—A comedian once said that "righteous people sleep better, but the wicked seem to enjoy their waking hours more." Even a *frum* Jew who is totally committed to the Torah may suffer from a nagging feeling that he is giving up all the joy and pleasure enjoyed by those who disregard the Torah. It pays to remind ourselves that there is a World to Come in which Divine justice gives every person what he deserves. And it pays to take note that even in this world, the supposed joy of the irreligious is largely illusory.

To take the extreme case, film stars and rock musicians have wealth, fame, and virtually no moral boundaries, yet their lives are filled with misery and tragedy. But even among more normal folk, the loss of a sense of meaningful existence and purpose, the absence of bedrock values to impart to children, the breakdown of the family, and the increase in so many kinds of social pathology all highlight the emptiness of life without Torah.

A Gallup poll surveyed the happiness and wellbeing of different faith groups in the United States. It should not surprise us that the happiest group in America is "Very Religious Jews." The truly wicked will surely be punished (here or in the hereafter), but the righteous (even if we are imperfectly so) are rewarded both in the future and in the here and now.

ח. יהודה בן טבאי ושמעון בן שטח קבלו מהם יהודה בן טבאי אומר אל תעש עצמך כעורכי הדינין וכשיהיו בעלי דינים עומדים לפניך יהיו בעיניך כרשעים וכשנפטרים מלפניך יהיו בעיניך כזכאין כשקבלו עליהם את הדין.

Mishnah 8. Yehudah ben Tabbai and Shimon ben Shetach received from them. Yehudah ben Tabbai says: Do not make yourself like a lawyer; and when parties to a lawsuit stand before you, let them be in your eyes as wicked; and when they go away from you let them be in your eyes as innocent, if they have accepted the verdict upon themselves.

This is advice (and warning) to judges, though Rav Yisrael Salanter pointed out that we are all like judges in our everyday decision-making, so there might well be practical applications of this Mishnah for us non-judges too.

"Do not make yourself like a lawyer"—The judge should not suggest (or even hint) to one of the litigants an argument he could make to win the case. The Talmud tells how Rabbi Yochanan advised a relative of a legal loophole to avoid making certain payments to the relative's step-mother, but then regretted having transgressed this Mishnah, even though Rabbi Yochanan was *not* judging the case. The Talmud concludes that it is permitted to give such advice if advising a relative (only), but even then, an *adam chashuv* (a distinguished person, i.e., a *talmid chacham*) should not do so.

"When parties to a lawsuit stand before you, let them be in your eyes as wicked"—Many people who shy away from accepting gossip nevertheless assume that someone claiming to be a victim must be telling the truth about the alleged victimizer. Many of us so easily accept as true any media accounts of wrongdoing, claims of couples going through a divorce, allegations of child abuse, and complaints against parents, teachers, and co-workers, that it pays to develop a healthy suspicion that there may be much more (or much less!) to the story than meets the eye.

Over the years, I have done a bit of marriage counseling (almost never by choice), and after listening separately to the husband and wife, I sometimes asked, "Are you sure the two of you are married to each other?" Even honest people end up twisting truth when they are emotionally involved, all the more so those whose honesty is suspect.

"When they go away from you, let them be in your eyes as innocent"—If you are a judge in a civil suit, or a teacher dealing with an unreasonable parent, after it's over, try to put any negative feelings aside. Whatever the litigant or parent said or did, assume they were under the control of powerful emotions, and with the case closed it's time to move on.

ט. שמעון בן שטח אומר הוי מרבה לחקור את העדים והוי זהיר
בדבריך שמא מתוכם ילמדו לשקר.

Mishnah 9. Shimon ben Shetach says: Engage in much examination of the witnesses, and be careful with your words, lest through them they learn to lie.

"Examination" includes a teacher or parent questioning a child, or even seeking information from a co-worker or fellow committee member. As gentle as you will be in asking questions, remain aware that some people are careless with facts or substitute imagination for reality. Children are especially blessed with active imaginations, but even adults often confuse assumptions with facts. A friend might say, "Yaakov went home after work" when he really means, "I saw Yaakov leave work, and he usually goes straight home."

"Lest through them they learn to lie"—The drift of a judge's questions may give the witness a clue as to the "correct" answer, even though it is untrue. Even where no dishonesty is intended, adults have been wrongly imprisoned for allegedly abusing pre-school children, based on evidence obtained by psychologists unconsciously coaching children to give the desired testimony.

Though not a "lie," this Mishnah is also a reminder to take great care in presenting a halachic question or asking advice from a *talmid chacham*. Omitting a seemingly minor detail may result in a different (and incorrect) halachic ruling, and someone seeking advice who makes it clear what he hopes to hear may find the *talmid chacham* giving it to him. I always admired one of my congregants who would preface his halachic questions by saying, "I have a *she'eilah* (question), but I'm not asking for a *heter* (leniency)."

י. שמעיה ואבטליון קבלו מהם שמעיה אומר אהב את המלאכה
ושנא את הרבנות ואל תתודע לרשות.

Mishnah 10. Shmayah and Avtalyon received from them. Shmayah says: Love work, and hate authority, and don't become close to the ruling authorities.

Sefarim and teachers of *mussar* speak extensively of the pitfalls of *kavod* (honor) and status-seeking, but for some reason they do not warn us so much about the natural desire for *power*—to be the person who gives orders and not the person who must take orders from others. This Mishnah teaches us as to how to deal with three different power relationships: If someone else has the power, if you have the power, or if you can be close (e.g., an assistant) to the one with power.

"Love work" (literally, "Love *the* work")—Many years ago, at a meeting of the *hanhalah* (administration) of Baltimore's Yeshivas Ner Yisroel, the Rosh Yeshiva, Rav Ruderman, wanted to make a rule outlawing radios in the student dormitories. The Mashgiach, Rav Kronglass, opposed the idea, arguing that besides the difficulties in enforcing the rule, the new "forbidden fruit" might encourage some students who had never done so to bring in radios.

Since Rav Ruderman was the boss, the rule was made. And to inform the students of the new rule, the job fell to: Rav Kronglass.

Rav Kronglass's *talmid* (Rav Gershon Weiss) told me: "The Mashgiach gave such a *shmuess*, you would have thought banning radios was his personal pet project for the year."

In working for a shul, school, or tzedakah organization, some volunteers will do certain jobs that suit them, but not other jobs that may be much more necessary. And if their preferred plan is voted down, they may refuse to do anything at all.

Chazal say that Chanoch was a shoemaker, and on every stitch he would unify the Divine presence and say, "Blessed be the Name of His Glorious Kingdom forever." Rav Yisrael Salanter taught that this should not be taken literally, for such holy meditations would cheat Chanoch's customers by diverting his attention from the work at hand. Rather, it means that Chanoch would give his full attention to every stitch, doing his job as expertly as he could, and his focus on doing the job that was his *itself* was a unification of the Divine presence and a proclaiming of "Blessed be the Name…"

"Hate authority"—This does not mean to hate those in positions of authority, but that we should hate being in a position of authority ourselves. Also note that it does not say to refuse to *accept* a position of authority. If it is a position with the power to guide a Torah institution or community, and you are the best person available, you may have an obligation to accept it. But since "power corrupts," how will you keep yourself from being corrupted?

(How can power corrupt truly good people? Consider two *talmidei chachamim* who partner to open a yeshiva, but after a time find themselves differing over matters of policy. Each one believes his approach is best for the *talmidim* and that his partner's approach will have deleterious effects. If it was a question of personal gain, each would willingly give in to the other, but how can he give in when the lives and souls of all the *talmidim* are at stake? *Machlokes* ensues and the yeshiva closes down, as, sadly, we have seen happen more than once.)

There is no foolproof protection, but an important step, the Mishnah tells us, is to *hate* having authority over others. Sometimes one must take the position of being in charge, and he must use his power to the full extent required (Shaul HaMelech failed because he shied away from asserting his authority when required). But he should try to at least feel uncomfortable giving orders and making demands, and part of him should always feel unworthy to hold a position of authority over others.

"And don't become close to the ruling authorities"—A simple worker who does his job whole-heartedly can live successfully; so can a powerful boss if he can develop the attitude discussed in the previous paragraph. But one power relationship that is almost sure to destroy us, and against which there is no defense, is to be an assistant or hanger-on to someone who truly does have serious power.

Shaul HaMelech was afflicted with anxiety that caused him to believe that David was plotting against him and that his own court was in league with David. Do'eg HaEdomi, wishing to please his sovereign, revealed that the Kohanim had given David food and a weapon. Do'eg knew that the Kohanim had acted in innocence, but the king commanded his guards to execute them as rebels. They bravely refused, so the king told Do'eg to kill them, and Do'eg, not wishing to refuse the king, committed mass murder on those he knew were innocent.

Power corrupts, but even the corrupted boss has some sort of conscience; however, the assistant to the powerful ends up negating his own free will in order to please the one in charge, and he will commit crimes he would not dream of doing for personal benefit.

Charles Colson, special counsel to President Richard Nixon and one of those convicted in the Watergate scandal, famously said that "he would walk over his grandmother for Nixon." The desire to please the powerful is so strong that, as the Mishnah cautions, the only way to resist is to keep one's distance in the first place.

יא. אבטליון אומר חכמים הזהרו בדבריכם שמא תחובו חובת
גלות ותגלו למקום מים הרעים וישתו התלמידים הבאים
אחריכם וימותו ונמצא שם שמים מתחלל.

Mishnah 11. Avtalyon says: Sages, be careful with your words,
lest you become liable to the obligation of exile, and be exiled
to a place of harmful waters; and students who come after you
will drink and die, with the result that the name of Heaven will
be desecrated.

Clearly this is a metaphor, but a metaphor for what? Chazal themselves apply this to Antignos of Socho, whose teaching, "Do not be like servants who serve the master for the sake of receiving a reward," was misunderstood by his students (or his students' students) as denying any Divine reward for fulfilling mitzvos, and "harmful waters" are a metaphor for the poison of heresy.

Apt as Chazal's application is, it leaves a couple of points unexplained: In what way is the Sage "exiled," and why should Antignos' students' misunderstanding mean that the *teacher* was exiled to a place of heresy? And if the waters are poisonous, how does the teacher drink without being harmed?

We might therefore suggest the following: Among great Torah thinkers and teachers, there are always some who are outside the mainstream (this is *not* a criticism). Rav Samson Raphael Hirsch, Rav Yisrael Salanter, the Satmar Rebbe, Rav Yoel Teitelbaum, and the *Rambam* in an earlier generation, all held and taught certain views that differed from those of the majority of their contemporaries, and their teachings are important contributions to Torah thought. But when a teacher is outside the mainstream, a student's misunderstanding will likely not be corrected by what we might call "peer review."

If *talmidim* in a mainstream Lithuanian-style yeshiva misunderstand their *rebbi*'s teaching on an important point of *hashkafah* (Torah worldview), they eventually learn that *rebbeim* and *talmidim* in similar yeshivas think very differently, leading them to go back to their *rebbi* for clarification or, if he has passed away, to modify their understanding based on what seems to be the consensus.

But if the *rebbi* and his yeshiva are considered "different" (by others) or "unique" (by his own *talmidim*), then the opinions and arguments of "outsiders" carry little weight. We see this among Breslover and Lubavitcher Chassidim, and also in some non-Chassidic yeshivas, especially in some smaller ones where there is only one *rebbi* whose *talmidim* are devoted to him. In such cases, a *talmid* who misunderstands will not revise his thinking based on what "outsiders" say, and may remain with a serious error in *hashkafah* or practical halachah.

(Note: This is in no way meant to imply that *rebbeim* outside the mainstream or their yeshivas are inferior. To study under giants like Rav Yisrael Salanter or the Satmar Rebbe would be a *ben Torah*'s dream! But the point here is that unique teachers can more easily end up being misunderstood.)

Based on this, the "exile" means to end up alone ("exiled") from the mainstream. "Harmful waters" are teachings that are dangerous if misunderstood (which of course pose no danger to the teacher who "drinks," because he knows what he means). But such Sages must choose their words with extra care, lest the students make a serious error that cannot be corrected, and the name of Heaven desecrated.

יב. הלל ושמאי קבלו מהם. הלל אומר הוי מתלמידיו של אהרן אוהב שלום ורודף שלום אוהב את הבריות ומקרבן לתורה.

Mishnah 12. Hillel and Shammai received from them. Hillel says: Be of the disciples of Aharon: Love peace and pursue

*peace, love human beings [beriyos; literally, "creations"] and
bring them close to the Torah.*

The Gemara says that Avraham Avinu had a set place (*makom kavua*)
for prayer. The Gemara also says that if we make a set place for prayer,
in Heaven they call us "*talmidim* of Avraham Avinu." In a related vein,
one of the Gerrer Rebbes wrote that Avraham's willingness to sacrifice
his son is what gave his descendants the power of *mesirus nefesh* (self-
sacrifice) through the generations.

We see then, that the early *tzaddikim's* spiritual achievements make it
easier for us to follow them, and that when we do follow them, we are in
some way considered to be their disciples. This means that besides the
intrinsic value of the mitzvah act, we can hope to have the *tzaddik* put in
a good word for us in Heaven; and when we eventually go to the "yeshiva
on high," we can hope to be united with our great *rebbeim*.

"Love peace and pursue peace"—Just about everyone thinks they love
peace, but "pursuing" peace—taking the first step to make peace even if
the other fellow is at fault—is less common. Many a peace-lover charitably
thinks that "surely, as soon as the other guy lets me have my way/agrees
I'm right/sincerely apologizes/does what I think he should, I'll make up
with him." "No justice, no peace" is not the battle-cry of *frum* organiza-
tions, but it does describe the attitude of too many *frum* individuals, with
"justice" being defined as whatever that individual happens to desire.

"Love human beings"—But why should we love everyone, and how
might we develop that love? Perhaps Hillel hints at the answer by using
the word *beriyos* (creations). Handwritten letters from *talmidei chachamim* of generations past are auctioned off for thousands of dollars.
How much more should we treasure Hashem's unique work of art that is
every human being, creations made in the *tzelem Elokim* (image of G-d)?
To think about this, and practice looking at our friends as if each one was
a Masterwork with a capital M, is a valuable first step.

"And bring them close to the Torah"—This is the source of the term
"*kiruv*" (bringing close), and it can refer both to attracting Jews who
are not-yet mitzvah observant, and bringing those who are already
observant that much closer.

Loving peace and pursuing peace are obviously closely related, and the same is true for loving human beings and bringing them close to Torah. If you love someone, you want the best for them in material things (which is why the Sages of the Gemara offer advice on medical matters and on making a living) and also in spiritual things, and *kiruv* is a natural result of love. But perhaps Hillel is also teaching us something more.

A Jewish woman who was not mitzvah-observant was befriended by a *kiruv*-oriented couple who regularly invited her for Shabbos meals. She became close to them and greatly valued their friendship. One day she told them that, after thinking it over, she decided that Orthodoxy was not for her. The Shabbos invitations ceased, the couple drew away from her, and she told me that she felt cheated. The "friendship" was like that of a used-car salesman pushing a product—nothing more.

Hillel is telling us: Don't befriend someone *in order* to sell them Yiddishkeit. Befriend them because you are a disciple of Aharon, bring them closer to Torah as a natural result of the friendship, but have the friendship not be based on their accepting what you have to offer. In any case, sincerity is much more effective, and we should not try to bring Jews closer to *Toras emes* in ways that are not *emes* themselves.

יג. הוא היה אומר נגיד שמא אבד שמיה ודלא מוסיף יסף ודלא
יליף קטלא חייב ודאשתמש בתגא חלף.

Mishnah 13. He used to say: He who seeks a name [fame] loses his name. He who does not increase, decreases. He who does not [i.e., refuses to] teach deserves death. And he who uses the crown [of Torah for personal benefit] will fade away.

"He who seeks a name," the person who seeks to make a name for himself, "loses his name"—status seekers and social climbers are recognized as such by others, and often end up becoming the object of their scorn. But if that is the only meaning of this Mishnah, it should have said, "He who seeks a name loses it." What is meant by "loses *his* name"?

Picture someone entering politics advocating a program that reflect his beliefs, but who is not elected because his program is unpopular with the voters. He might then embark on a campaign to educate voters and persuade them to change their views, but more often he ends up changing his program in order to win the next election. It used to be shameful for politicians to admit they were sacrificing principle for expediency, but Bill Clinton's campaign manager Dick Morris was open about Clinton's "triangulation strategy" to win re-election.

It would therefore seem that the ideal political candidate has no views of his own but simply adopts whatever view is most electable, changing principles as easily as he changes his clothes. When President George Bush Sr. was asked by a friend to take a few days to figure out where he wanted to take the country, Bush said, in exasperation, "Oh, you mean the vision thing."

Abandonment of principle is not confined to politicians. We all know people whose views change from year to year according to the fashion, including (for *frum* Jews) the *frum* fashion. More than not having views of their own, in a sense they cease to be their own individual persons, and they become empty shells, filled and refilled with the ephemeral and the trendy. The status-and-popularity-seeker, seeking to make a name for himself, loses *his* name—those aspects of mind and personality that make him the special individual he is.

"HE WHO DOES NOT increase, decreases"—If we are not spending time learning, we are spending time forgetting, but the lesson extends to many other areas of Torah living as well. "The path of life is upward for the wise, so that he may veer away from the underworld (*she'ol*) beneath" (*Mishlei* 15:24). As many dieters discover, maintaining one's ideal weight can be harder than trying to lose another pound. So too with spiritual progress: the feelings of accomplishment that accompany each step forward encourage us to take yet another, while stagnation leads to deterioration.

Others translate this phrase as "He who does not increase comes to an end" (*yasef* related to *sof*/ending or *ne'esaf*/gathered in), meaning that he may die. This is not a punishment, as in the Mishnah's next clause ("He who does not teach *deserves* death"), but a result of his emptying his life of meaning. The Gemara says that when a student moved from the Torah metropolis of Pumbedisa to the nearby town of Bei Kuvi, his *rebbi* doubted that the student would live out the year. We are here in this world to make progress. If someone no longer progresses, and all the more so if he deteriorates, Heaven may bring his life to an end as a blessing for him.

(It's important to note that progress is measured by different yard-sticks as we age or take on more responsibilities. For a young woman who davens three times daily who then becomes a mother, it sometimes might be progress if she manages to daven at all.)

"HE WHO DOES NOT [refuses to] teach deserves death." We say a *berachah* that Hashem is "*melamed Torah l'amo*—He teaches [present tense!] Torah to His people." When we teach others we are, at that moment, serving as His agents to transmit His Torah. Teaching is more than merely one aspect of *talmud Torah*; *Chumash* never explicitly commands us to learn but only implies it with the words "*V'shinantam...v'limad'tem*—And you shall *teach*." One who refuses to teach is comparable to a man receiving a large gift from the king with the command that he share it with others but refuses to do so.

"And he who uses the crown will fade away"—The Gemara says that one who holds a *sefer Torah* with his bare hands loses the mitzvah (learning or *hagbah*) he performed with it. We see here that treating the Torah in a manner that is not respectful negates the learning, and so too, using one's Torah stature for personal gain empties the person of his Torah content. He has knowledge, but the light of Torah in him has gone out.

The word *chalaf* ("fade away") is like the word *machlif* (exchange). Although it may appear that his Torah knowledge is unchanged, this person has actually exchanged *Toras Hashem* for something else—something that cannot endure to nourish the soul in the long term.

יד. הוא היה אומר אם אין אני לי מי לי וכשאני לעצמי מה אני ואם לא עכשו אימתי.

Mishnah 14. He used to say: If I am not for myself, who is for me? And if I am for myself, what am I? And if not now, when?

Without Divine assistance, we cannot succeed in anything in life: not in making a living, Torah learning, mitzvah performance, or raising a family. To merit that assistance, we must pray for it, and after praying, we must *act*.

In daily davening, we ask Hashem to teach us *chukei chaim* (the laws of life, how to live), and to put into our hearts the ability and desire to learn and teach and do. But this must be followed (preferably right after davening) by applying ourselves to spend time learning, if possible a bit of teaching, and to ask what more might we do in the way of action this day. When we daven the berachah of *Hashivenu* (return us in complete repentance), we should consider what small step we might take to help us get there, and so too for everything for which we pray. "If I am not for myself," I cannot expect Hashem's help to be there for me.

And after committing myself to the task at hand, and even if it is going well, I must never forget that I need Hashem's help, and that I must keep asking for it. "If I am for myself (without Divine assistance), what am I?"

"And if not now"—The young man or woman says, "When I finish school, then I will strive to become the person I aspire to be." The graduate says, "When I get a job" or "when I marry" or "when I have children" or "when I make enough money" or "when I retire," etc. Even if I put off fulfilling my resolution for only a short time, unforeseen circumstances can arise, or my original burst of enthusiasm may wane without warning.

Before our ancestors left Egypt, they were commanded to eat the Pesach offering in haste, and Rav Tzadok of Lublin wrote that this teaches us not to put off beginning a new form of serving Hashem. I may have what appear to be good reasons to delay, but as the Alter from Novardok put it: "Set aside all your 'tomorrows' for the sake of acting today, lest you end up setting aside all your 'todays' for the sake of a 'tomorrow' that never comes."

טו. שמאי אומר עשה עשה תורתך קבע אמור מעט ועשה הרבה והוי מקבל את כל האדם בסבר פנים יפות.

Mishnah 15. Shammai says: Make your Torah study fixed [a fixed time]; say little and do much; and receive every person with a cheerful countenance.

These are three well-known Torah teachings, though one reason why they are well-known is because Shammai taught them! Might they all be connected in some way?

Of the hundreds of disagreements between Beis Hillel and Beis Shammai, the lion's share concern *gezeiros*, Rabbinic safeguards to protect Torah laws, with Beis Shammai almost always taking the stricter view. We do not know the underlying principles that led them to take their respective positions, but it is at least reasonable to suggest that Shammai was more concerned about human frailty and the need to guard against crossing the line into spiritual self-destruction. With this in mind, we can recognize that same theme in this Mishnah.

"Make your Torah study fixed"—Yeshiva-men Reuven and Shimon both plan to get in some serious Torah learning during their upcoming *bein hazmanim* vacations. Reuven says, "I'm going to learn as much as I can," while Shimon says, "Two hours of learning every day immediately after *Shacharis*, come what may." Even if Reuven planned on more than two hours, very often it is Shimon whose resolution will be kept. Having a fixed time for *talmud Torah* shows respect for the mitzvah, and given human frailty, it is also more likely to succeed.

"Say little and do much"—Every now and then, someone will ask when they might be able to meet with me to consider how they might do more in the way of Torah learning or mitzvah observance. If at all possible, I respond: "How about meeting right now?" This is because experience has taught me that if the meeting is put off by even a day, it is likely that the meeting will never take place.

A statement of Chazal made famous by *Mesillas Yesharim* is: "Many are the obstacles between here and the River Gichon." These obstacles include not only unforeseen problems, but the nature of enthusiasm to wane without warning (see Mishnah 14 above).

If I tell my friend that "I'll be happy to help with your committee/program/project," he will rely on me, and when I don't follow through, he will be upset with both the unfinished work and the knowledge that he could have asked someone else.

There is also another, deeper problem, which is that some people get into the habit of confusing "agreeing to help" with actually helping. They volunteer for all sorts of worthy causes but end up doing very little, yet they pat themselves on the back for their public-spiritedness on behalf of the *klal*. Recognizing how fragile our idealism can be keeps us from allowing words to take the place of acts.

"And receive every person with a cheerful countenance"—Ideally, we should do much more, up to and including "Love thy neighbor as thyself." But human frailty being what it is, what is there we can demand of ourselves that has a reasonable chance of succeeding? Shammai's answer is: If not love, we can at least greet every person with a smile.

This is something you can practice: starting with a mirror, moving on to your spouse, and eventually even co-workers and in-laws. I heard from a *talmid* of pre-war Slabodka that in the yeshiva they studied how to say "Good morning!" with enthusiasm and a glad-to-see-you smile.

The Alter from Slabodka also taught that the three words of "*sever panim yafos*" ("cheerful countenance") are three distinct aspects of greeting. "*Sever*," related to the word *sevara*, means to look thoughtful, i.e., interested; "*panim*" ("face") means to turn your face to *look* at the other person (it's surprising how many people don't); and "*yafos*" means to do so with a smile.

טז. רבן גמליאל היה אומר עשה לך רב והסתלק מן הספק ואל תרבה לעשר אמדות.

Mishnah 16. Rabban Gamliel used to say: Make for yourself a rav and depart from uncertainty; and do not give more tithes by estimating [or: do not be in the habit of tithing by estimating].

Besides the other benefits of having a *rebbi* (see above, Mishnah 6), there is also the freedom from uncertainty in both practical halachah and many of life's decisions.

In practical halachah: When *poskim* (halachic authorities) differ on a question of Biblical law (*d'Oraysa*) and no consensus has yet emerged, I would usually have to play it safe by following the stricter view (which itself is not always possible). But if I have a competent *rav*, he has the status of "the judge who will be in those days," and I am permitted to follow his ruling, even if his is the lenient view.

In decision-making: As I mentioned (Mishnah 6), when I had to make an important decision, my *rebbeim* would help me evaluate the various pros and cons so that I could reach my own conclusions. But even with their help, I sometimes remained in doubt and could not reach a decision. On one such occasion, I said: "I understand the Rosh Yeshiva does not wish to make the decision for me, but if the Rosh Yeshiva would have to decide, what would he say?" He then gave me his opinion (as it happened, not the one I was hoping for!), and I said to myself: "I've done the best I can. Whether the Rosh Yeshiva's advice was right or wrong, when I am judged after 120 years, I'll be able to say that I acted according to the Torah, the best I knew how.

(It turned out he was right, of course.)

"Tithing"—Some understand this to be a halachic concern—that the excess separated will not have the halachic status of *maaser*—but if that is the sole point of the Mishnah, it is strange that it is part of a Mishnah in *Avos*. But if we translate it as "do not be in the habit of tithing by estimating," it is teaching a more general lesson connected to "Make for yourself a *rav* and depart from uncertainty." The lesson is: A careful, meticulous person tends to be precise in all he does; a person who is not meticulous tends to become careless and uncertain, and his character weakens.

Someone who responds amen to a *berachah* without knowing what *berachah* he has heard is said to have uttered an "*amen yesomah*" ("orphaned amen"). The Gemara comments that, regarding someone who says an *amen yesomah*, "*yihiyu banav yesomim*," (his children will be orphans). But surely saying an orphaned *amen* is not a capital crime!

Rav Yosef Leib Bloch explained: The man who habitually responds to *berachos* without knowing what he is responding to is not a man who plans his actions and then follows through with vigorous, full-blooded resolve. The habit of *uncertainty* (which is the connection between the two parts of this Mishnah) becomes ingrained, fashioning those people we know who seem unable to ever make up their minds or who follow the advice of whoever spoke to them last. His "children will be orphans" emotionally, without a strong father figure to guide them.

יז. שמעון בנו אומר כל ימי גדלתי בין החכמים ולא מצאתי
לגוף טוב משתיקה. ולא המדרש הוא העיקר אלא המעשה. וכל
המרבה דברים מביא חטא.

Mishnah 17. His son Shimon said: all my days I grew up among the Sages, and I found nothing better for the body than silence. And study is not the main thing, but the deed. And all who speak much bring about sin.

We all know about not speaking gossip and even *devarim beteilim* (idle chatter), and the need to "guard your tongue" or *machsom l'fi* ("a muzzle for my mouth," with its unfortunate bovine connotation). All these are *negatives*, things *not* to do, but the *Rambam* writes of silence as a positive *middah* (character trait): "*L'olam yarbeh adam b'shtikah*," as Rabbi Shimon does in this Mishnah. What does the Mishnah mean, then, when it makes a positive assertion regarding proper speech?

To be comfortable with silence is to be in control of oneself; we all know people who cannot sit quietly without feeling ill at ease, and who cannot let a friend finish a thought without interrupting. To be comfortable with silence engenders peace of mind and allows for the sort of reflection that is so rare today. It also gives us the calm to consider what to say and how to say it, saving us from many troubles: "He who guards his mouth and tongue guards his soul from troubles" (*Mishlei*), or as the saying goes, "Caution: engage brain before putting mouth in gear."

"Nothing better for the body" includes both physical and emotional health, and material well-being. A *bachur* asked the great Mashgiach, Rav Yechezkel Levenstein, how to deal with anxiety, and the Mashgiach replied: "*Redt nisht*—Don't speak." Stress brings illness and often shortens our lives. The *middah* of silence takes work to develop, but it is well-worth the investment of time and effort.

"And all who speak much bring about sin"—"All" would include the person speaking on a subject that is worthwhile and even necessary, and (apparently) even when speaking words of Torah. Granted that more speaking increases the likelihood of forbidden speech creeping in, but to say that this is true of *all* who speak excessively would seem to be somewhat excessive.

Perhaps we can understand this with the *Maharal*'s ideas (in *Nesivos Olam*) that

1. every person's mind contains a certain amount of wisdom and a certain amount of foolishness (the difference between wise men and fools being the relative proportions of each),
2. foolishness in the mind is not crystallized until it is expressed in word or deed.

The silent man's wisdom is fully formed, while his foolishness is more potential than actual. Therefore, even when we say something that needs saying (which equals wisdom, of Torah or of the world), anything *extra* automatically contains a mixture of wisdom and foolishness, and that foolishness is opening the door to sin (although sin will not necessarily enter every time).

יח. רבן שמעון בן גמליאל אומר על שלשה דברים העולם קיים על האמת ועל הדין ועל השלום שנאמר אמת ומשפט שלום שפטו בשעריכם.

Mishnah 18. Rabban Shimon ben Gamliel said: On three things the world endures: on emes, on din, and on shalom, as it is said, "Truth and a judgment of peace, judge in your gates."

We learned in Mishnah 2 that the world *stands* on three things (Torah, *avodah*, and acts of kindness), meaning that those three are the purpose of life and the pillars holding up the structure of our existence. Here, Rabban Shimon teaches that even if we are devoted to those three, in order to succeed, we must add the three ingredients of *emes*, *din*, and *shalom*, each in its proper measure according to the situation.

For example, *lashon hara* is forbidden (*din*), even if the report is true (*emes*).

In a *din Torah*, litigants are often encouraged to reach an amicable settlement among themselves (*shalom* rather than *din*) but a *beis din* usually cannot compel a *pesharah* (compromise), and *din* will trump *shalom*.

If certain individuals are misleading the community, we are often required to fight for *emes* (*emes* rather than *shalom*), but when informing others of the harm being done, we must carefully follow the halachic guidelines of *sefer Chafetz Chaim* (*din* takes priority).

Emes often requires a *ben Torah* to maintain a higher standard of mitzvah observance (*mitzvah min ha'muvchar* or even *chassidus*), but family or communal harmony (*shalom*) sometimes requires that he not do so, in which case it is vital to know what is actually halachically required (*din*).

"Just as it is a mitzvah to say something that will be listened to, so is it a mitzvah not to say something that will not be listened to" (*din* rather than *emes*).

רבי חנניא בן עקשיא אומר. רצה הקדוש ברוך הוא לזכות את
ישראל לפיכך הרבה להם תורה ומצות. שנאמר ה' חפץ למען
צדקו יגדיל תורה ויאדיר.

Rabbi Chananya ben Akashia says, "The Holy One, blessed be He, desired to give merit to Israel, therefore He gave them Torah and mitzvos in abundance. As it is said: 'Hashem desired for the sake of his righteousness, [therefore] He made the Torah great and mighty.'"

This Mishnah is in *Masechta Makkos*, but it is always learned at the end of each chapter of *Avos*. But don't we know this already? Each mitzvah gives merit (reward); the more mitzvos, the more merit, so what is the Mishnah teaching that is new?

Perhaps the Mishnah is teaching more than its simple translation reveals.

The *Rambam* explains it to us in his commentary on the Mishnah: Although there is reward for every mitzvah, the entrance requirement to *Olam Haba* (the World to Come) is to perform *one* mitzvah flawlessly, in deed and in intent, *one* time. Since different mitzvos appeal to different people, an abundance of mitzvos increases the odds that sooner or later we will do at least *one* mitzvah flawlessly and thereby merit *Olam Haba*.

A new idea, isn't it?

We begin each chapter of *Avos* with the Mishnah from *Sanhedrin* reminding us that we are already a spiritual success (see above, "*Kol Yisrael*" etc.), and we need not feel overwhelmed by all the additional demands found in *Avos*. For this same reason, we end each chapter with this Mishnah from *Makkos* to remind us that each additional demand is another opportunity to enter the eternal winner's circle.

This teaching is also a great *chizuk*, a source of encouragement in difficult times. No matter how badly the day is going, and no matter how poorly you judge your own level of spiritual accomplishment, you never know when the moment will arrive that you will do *your* mitzvah (e.g., perhaps helping out another person when you are not in the mood, *because* the day is going so badly) in that special way that will cause the angels to break out in thunderous applause as you earn your ticket to *Olam Haba*.

Chapter Two

א. רבי אומר איזו היא דרך ישרה שיבור לו האדם כל שהיא
תפארת לעושיה ותפארת לו מן האדם. והוי זהיר במצוה קלה
כבחמורה שאין אתה יודע מתן שכרן של מצות. והוי מחשב
הפסד מצוה כנגד שכרה ושכר עבירה כנגד הפסדה. הסתכל
בשלשה דברים ואין אתה בא לידי עברה. דע מה למעלה ממך
עין ראה ואזן שומעת וכל מעשיך בספר נכתבים.

*Mishnah 1. Rebbi says, what is a proper path [derech] that
a person should select for himself? Whatever is tiferes
[beautiful or suited] for himself and tiferes [brings honor or
esteem] from other people. And be as careful with a minor
mitzvah as with a major one, for you do not know the reward
given for mitzvos. Look carefully at three things and you will
not come to the hands of sin: Know what is above you—an Eye
that sees, an Ear that hears, and all your deeds are written in
a book.*

Rav Isser Zalman Meltzer taught in the great yeshivas of
Lithuania and Eretz Yisrael for over half a century. In his later
years, a young Torah scholar visited him and asked a *kashya*
(difficult question) in Gemara. When Rav Isser Zalman gave his answer,
the young man said, "But that's just the standard answer they give in
the yeshivas" (as apparently, he was hoping to hear something original).
The old sage replied, "Yes, it is the standard answer, and I made it so,
fifty years ago."

We are all familiar with the idea of a *derech*, the need for an individual path to serving Hashem and making spiritual progress, and Klal Yisrael has accepted many different *derachim* such as *mussar*, Chassidus, Kabbalah, Philosophy, etc. But we are familiar with the idea only because *Avos* taught it to us in this chapter—here and in Mishnah 13—that there are indeed different *derachim* suited to different people.

(Every yeshiva man is also aware of different *derachim* in learning, but that is probably not the subject of this Mishnah.)

Besides being raised or choosing to follow the *derech* of a particular group (such as Chassidus or *mussar*), there is also (or at least should be) the conscious choice of a particular *derech* for the *individual*. This most often involves choosing which areas of *avodas Hashem* to concentrate on and in what order.

For example, one person might decide to work this year on davening with *kavanah* and avoiding *lashon hara*, and after a year or two of some success (hopefully!), working on developing a love for *chessed*. Another person might make this year's priority strengthening diligence in Torah learning and maintaining an attitude of *simchah*, going on from there to work on *bitachon* and *menuchas ha'nefesh* (peace of mind). Each person must find what works for them, and one size definitely does not fit all.

However, the Mishnah warns us that in choosing our *derech*, we must take care that it be *tiferes* for ourselves and *tiferes* in the eyes of other people.

Tiferes for ourselves means choosing a *derech* that is suited to the unique individual each one of us is. The Vilna Gaon taught that some people have a *mazal* that they are destined to shed blood (!), but they have free will to choose whether to become a murderer, a *mohel*, or a *shochet* (or a surgeon?). If he tries to stay away from a profession involving blood, he will not succeed, and the results may be disastrous.

Other examples: A *baalas teshuvah* from California married a *ben Torah*, and together they went to live in an ancient apartment in Meah Shearim. It did not turn out well.

A young man from a non-religious family became a chassid and completely cast aside his interest in political philosophy and sports. After a few years, he faced a crisis, as his old interests kept pulling at his heart and would not fade. Should he change to some form of Modern Orthodoxy or remain an unhappy chassid? Neither choice was satisfactory to him, so he made a third choice: He decided to remain a devoted chassid who also spent time in the world of political philosophy and the New York Mets.

While that would likely not be the best solution for everyone, many a *baal teshuvah* has found that rejecting old interests in art or music carries a cost, and finding the right balance (a balance that may change with the passing years) can be the key to spiritual success.

A teenager who is a sincere *ben Torah* decides to "work on himself" by resolving to refrain from all soda and candy. Laudable as his resolution may be, if his struggle to abstain from soda occupies his mind to the extent that it interferes with his learning, davening, and *simchas ha'chaim* (joy of life) week after week, perhaps selecting a different resolution would be more worthwhile.

"*Tiferes* from other people"—"Other people" obviously means those who share Torah values and have the wisdom to offer an educated opinion. First and foremost, this means a *rebbi* or at least a *talmid chacham* who knows you. It also includes *chaverim*, those currently in yeshiva or alumni who are *b'nei Torah*. In a letter of guidance to yeshiva students, the Chazon Ish wrote: "Not to act in a way that is different from one's *chaverim*, and to be exceedingly careful about this."

Why is this so important? In choosing a *derech*, there is always the danger of feeding one's own neurosis, like the shy and withdrawn student who decides to "work on" *shtikah* (maintaining silence) or the obsessive-compulsive who commits to extra care in hand-washing. I heard from a respected yeshiva *mashgiach* that in the days when unmarried students did not generally grow beards, the socially-awkward student who did grow a beard was a matter of great concern. More than one Orthodox man or family left the city to live on a farm with the most spiritual intentions, but being far from other *frum* Jews, ended up drifting away from mitzvah observance entirely.

What if, after careful consideration, I believe I must follow a certain *derech* that differs from the mainstream? Must I have the approval of a *rebbi* who himself may have a totally different *derech*? It depends: If your *rebbi* says, "I don't advise it, but it is a reasonable plan," then you have a right to go ahead if you truly believe it's best. But if the *rebbi* says, "no way," then listen to him for two reasons: (1) He's probably right; and (2) for *any* plan to succeed, you must have *siyata d'Shmaya* (Divine assistance), and you are unlikely to receive it if you go against your *rebbi*'s directive.

Caution: If, when consulting a *talmid chacham*, you give the impression that you've already made up your mind, he may offer encouragement (and implied approval), even when he thinks it's a bad idea. So do your best to make clear that you are looking for his opinion, not your own.

"And (or "but") be as careful with a minor mitzvah as a major one, for you do not know the reward given for mitzvos"—The Mishnah does not need to tell us that a chosen *derech* must not violate any halachah, but we might decide that our *derech* requires us to neglect certain mitzvos (e.g., davening with a minyan or devoting time to *chessed* or *kibbud av va'eim*) and that it is worth losing those mitzvos to gain the benefits of our *derech*. The Mishnah therefore warns us to avoid such trade-offs because we cannot know how much we lose by neglecting a mitzvah. Besides the Divine reward, each mitzvah affects the soul in ways unknown to us but which can have an impact, even in this world.

(As is often the case, the general rule may have exceptions. For instance, someone whose *derech* demands that he adhere to a strict daily schedule—experience having taught him that without such adherence, his productive day falls apart—may have to neglect certain mitzvah opportunities when they arise. But these decisions must be made carefully, and of course, without ever violating a halachah.)

"Look carefully at three things"—i.e., think about them. The Mishnah uses the word *histakel* ("Look carefully or intently"), meaning that we are to create a mental picture so that in our mind's eye we "see" the Eye, Ear, and Book. This was Rav Yisrael Salanter's program of *mussar b'hispaalus*—to make abstract truths come alive. For instance, I believe without question that on Rosh Hashanah my life hangs in the balance as Hashem decides my fate for the coming year, and yet I do not tremble as much as I did when a policeman once pulled me over for a traffic violation! *Histakel* is to meditate with the goal of making the truths of *emunah* real—to transform "belief" into concrete knowledge.

"And you will not come to the hands of sin"—In several places, Chazal indicate that the grip of a strong temptation is almost impossible to overcome (and perhaps the word "almost" should sometimes be deleted). Proper use of free will is therefore to do all we can to avoid temptation in the first place, in three ways:

1. Prayer, as we ask every day not to come *li'yedei nisayon*, "to the hands of challenge"
2. Avoidance of problematic situations, as we find in the laws of *yichud*
3. Constant awareness of the seeing Eye, listening Ear, and the Book we are inscribing with our deeds

"And all your deeds are written in a book"—After knowing that Hashem sees and hears, we have no doubt that He also remembers all that we do, so why the need to write our deeds down?

A simple understanding of Divine reward and punishment is that Hashem chooses to repay us for deeds good and bad, but we know there is more to it. Each mitzvah is a unique form of nourishment for the soul, while every transgression does spiritual harm; the eventual joy or suffering is to a large extent a direct result of what we have done to ourselves. "Deeds written" means that the deeds themselves are not merely in the past but have an ongoing permanent effect.

"In a book"—If our deeds were recorded on sheets of paper or shards of pottery, they would be just as permanent. Why are they recorded in a *book*?

Two answers. First: the *book* is a biography—of you.

If you prefer, imagine that Hollywood would make a film about your life story. Would it be a comedy or a tragedy? What would be the high and low points? Would it have a happy ending? Try thinking about your life story as a whole, with the goal being able to tell your family what it's about.

More than a mere retelling of many unrelated events, a biographer usually finds in his subject a particular theme running through the protagonist's life, e.g., how he or she faced daunting challenges and overcame (or did not overcome) them; how a man or woman with potential and opportunity fell prey to hubris, greed or lust, finally making (or not making) a comeback. If you cannot identify a unifying theme in your own story, perhaps you should consider creating one.

Second is something I wrote many years ago in an essay for wives and mothers, but the idea applies to men as well:

> *One feels a certain inner satisfaction when, after hours of sustained effort, one's home is finally spotlessly clean. But how shall a woman keep her enthusiasm alive when the very next week (or next day, for the fastidious) she must begin all over again? A similar difficulty faces every Jew: After a meal, we can all express heartfelt gratitude in Birkas Hamazon—once. But to repeat the identical words of Birkas Hamazon (or daily Shemoneh Esreh) each time as graciously as the first, day after day for decades? How can we keep today's fires burning brightly through all the identical tomorrows?*
>
> *The Mishnah in Avos answers: Today's mitzvah is not a mere repetition of yesterday's; it's a continuation. All good deeds are recorded and linked together to form a book, and each additional chapter signifies an entirely new level of achievement (the same is true for bad deeds, but that's another story). The modern knight-errant downs his 4,239th glass of beer with undiminished ardor, if he knows it will grant him immortality in the Guinness Book of World Records. Similarly (le'havdil, that is), each additional berachah recited, meal served, dish washed, or diaper changed is another mitzvah added to the top of the pile, building Heavenward a structure for eternity.*
>
> *In Heaven, we are all writing our own biographies, so why not take a sneak preview of some of your best chapters? Try computing the number of berachos or amens or meals you prepare or spills you wipe up over a lifetime, giving yourself some much-needed encouragement and providing incentives*

*to further increase your score. (Adapted from In Search of the
Jewish Woman, Feldheim 1984)*

ב. רבן גמליאל בנו של רבי יהודה הנשיא אומר יפה תלמוד תורה
עם דרך ארץ שיגיעת שניהם משכחת עון וכל תורה שאין עמה
מלאכה סופה בטלה וגוררת עון.

*Mishnah 2. Rabban Gamliel the son of Rabbi Yehudah HaNasi
says: Beautiful is Torah study accompanied by derech eretz,
for the exertion of both of them makes sin forgotten. And any
Torah [study] that is not accompanied by melachah [work], in
the end will come to nothing and lead to sin.*

Derech eretz in this Mishnah almost certainly means an occupation
(though we will see later that it may also include more), and Rabban
Gamliel seems to be saying that combining Torah study with an occupation is something we are supposed to do. But if so, why use the word,
"beautiful"? If it is an obligation, or at least a goal we should all strive to
achieve, why not say so? ("*Rabbi, should I make my kitchen kosher?*" "*Well,
my son, kashrus is a beautiful thing…*"—you get the idea.)

Furthermore, if all of us are to combine Torah study with an occupation, does this mean that every *bachur* in yeshiva (and every high-school
student) must also have a job? If there is such a halachah, why have we
never heard of it or practiced it?

The answer is: Try to imagine what it was like for Rabban Gamliel,
a Nasi (leader of the Jewish People in Eretz Yisrael) and son of a Nasi.
A great deal of his time was spent dealing with the ruling Roman
authorities, more time dealing with internal Jewish politics, communal
needs, tzedakah needs, and presiding over the Sanhedrin. Surely, he
would have preferred being able to devote all his time and attention to
Torah learning and teaching.

But he consoled himself, and all of us whose free time is limited by
parnassah and other obligations, by pointing out the blessings of being
busy: "exertion of both of them makes sin forgotten." Not that a serious
Torah learner should seek to be weighed down by other obligations; if

you could and truly would spend all your time studying, that would be wonderful. But if your situation includes the burden of making a living, recognize that there is also beauty in it and give thanks.

I wrote "*parnassah* and other obligations" for a reason. The term "*derech eretz*" sometimes means only working for a living, but if that is the meaning here, the Mishnah should not then have switched to *melachah* ("Torah that is not accompanied by *melachah*"), which does mean "work." But *derech eretz* ("the way of the land") refers to all our obligations as members of human society—family obligations, civic obligations, and making a living. Much of our time is taken up with these, and whatever is required of us, besides often having intrinsic mitzvah-value, it makes our limited time for Torah learning that much more precious and more beautiful.

וכל העוסקים עם הצבור יהיו עוסקים עמהם לשם שמים שזכות אבותם מסייעתם וצדקתם עומדת לעד ואתם מעלה אני עליכם שכר הרבה כאלו עשיתם.

And all who work for the community should work with them for the sake of Heaven, for [it is] the merit of their ancestors [that] helps them, whose righteousness lasts forever. But you, [Hashem says,] I will give you great reward, as if you had accomplished it.

Any mitzvah performed altruistically "for the sake of Heaven" is superior to the same mitzvah performed out of lesser motives. Why then does the Mishnah single out the need for idealism in community work?

I think it was Charles de Gaulle who said that "the cemeteries are filled with indispensable men." A single individual or a small group can be the pillars of the community by providing the necessary funding, guidance, or hard work that keeps the shul, school, or tzedakah organization going. But those individuals need to know: If they were not here, Hashem would have sent others to do the work (and perhaps given those others the wealth or talent instead of you). A community's success depends on factors besides ourselves, such as "the merit of ancestors," and our chief mitzvah contribution is therefore our *kavanah* (motivation and intent). If we have the right *kavanah*, Hashem then rewards us "as *if* you had accomplished it," because our *kavanah* is what makes this work our own.

ג. הוו זהירין ברשות שאין מקרבין לו לאדם אלא לצורך עצמן נראין כאוהבין בשעת הנאתן ואין עומדין לו לאדם בשעת דחקו.

Mishnah 3. Be cautious of the ruling authorities, for they befriend a man only for their own needs; they appear as friends while they have benefit, but do not stand by a man in his time of distress.

Shmayah (see above, Chapter 1, Mishnah 10) cautioned us to stay far from the ruling powers and their corrupting influence, and this applies even to Jewish rulers, as in the case of Shaul HaMelech. But what if circumstances require you to be close to the rulers? This applies not only in politics, but also in business and academia (including Torah institutions) or any setting with a hierarchy. Rabban Gamliel experienced this himself in his position as son and successor to the Nasi.

In all such cases, he tells us something new: People in charge, even *good* people in charge (with the exception of great *tzaddikim*) appear to be your friends more than they truly are and cannot be counted on in a crisis.

To repeat, this is *not* because they are necessarily bad people. Rather (to use the example of a political leader), the leader seeking to help his nation has a vision or plan how to do so. To succeed, he seeks to accumulate as much power as possible—for the best of reasons (though the corrupting power of the ego inevitably accompanies this)—and in his mind, doing whatever keeps him in power is synonymous with the good of the country. If you can help him, he cares about you like a narcissist cares about his wife—as one of his possessions giving him fulfillment. He does not intentionally deceive, but his friendship is only a product of what you do for him. If he no longer needs you, or if you need him and he must go out of his way to help, he will not hesitate to "throw you under the bus."

ה. הלל אומר אל תפרוש מן הצבור ואל תאמין בעצמך עד יום
מותך ואל תדין את חברך עד שתגיע למקומו ואל תאמר דבר
שאי אפשר לשמוע שסופו להשמע ואל תאמר לכשאפנה אשנה
שמא לא תפנה.

Mishnah 5. Hillel says: Do not separate from the community. And do not believe in [i.e., trust] yourself until the day of your death. And do not judge your fellow until you have reached his place. And do not say something that cannot be heard, for in the end it will be heard. And do not say, "When I will be free, I will study," for perhaps you will not be free.

"Do not separate from the community"—i.e., the community of Jews who both keep and respect the Torah. There are many reasons for this:

1. Hashem gave the Torah not to individuals but to Klal Yisrael as a whole, and there is extra Divine assistance given only to the community (e.g., the Gemara says that Hashem will not reject the *tefillah* of the *rabim*).
2. As the *Rambam* writes in *Hilchos De'os* (6:1), the way Hashem created us (a.k.a., human nature) is that we imitate the deeds and attitudes of our neighbors. Having friends and neighbors who are on a higher spiritual and lower material plane is an easy way to grow with virtually no effort.
3. Years ago, a member of the Conservative synagogue in Freehold, New Jersey, wanted to study some Torah, and he and I ended up learning together once a week. He and his family also took a few steps towards mitzvah observance. When he got a new job near Monsey, New York, he moved to Monsey, and I was worried that it might prove too great an adjustment for him and his family. However, within weeks, he was attending a *daf yomi* shiur, his wife soon put on a sheitel, and I when I last saw him, he had completed half of *Shas*. He had been a good man when he still

lived in Freehold, but entering a Torah-oriented social circle made him a great one.

4. The *Chovos Halevavos* writes that a major motivator for the good deeds we do is *shame*—that we don't want to look bad to our neighbors. (I think we can add that the absence of shame in today's world has had a huge impact on people's behavior.) If all my neighbors go to minyan and daily *shiurim*, I will too, and I am far less likely to if my neighbors don't.

   This is also one of many reasons to always daven in the same shul, as others will notice if you don't show up. As Rav Hutner is reported to have said, "Once a shtetl has two shuls, a man has the option of going to daven in neither one."

"And do not believe in yourself until the day of your death,"—i.e., remain humble and on guard, with all safeguards in place to avoid sin, even if you've withstood temptation all your life. Among the reasons why this is necessary:

1. The day may come when you are faced with some entirely new temptation, or a new variant on an old one ("I've never taken a dishonest dollar in my life, but to embezzle a dishonest million dollars, well...")

2. You may find yourself weakening when faced with some financial or medical crisis, or even a general personal mid-life crisis, and find yourself facing temptations undreamed of in years past.

3. Prolonged exposure to books or acquaintances who are filled with heresy, mockery, or cynicism toward Yiddishkeit can have a corrosive effect that may not surface for years but eventually causes complete spiritual ruination.

4. Old age is no guarantee. Late-life depression can strike anyone; older people find change an ordeal, and are sometimes less patient and more prone to anger than ever before. In the words of Rav Yehudah Leib Chasman, Mashgiach of Yeshivas Slabodka-Chevron: "I say that someone who in his younger years seeks a measure of *kavod*, in his older years will seek *kavod* without limit!"

"And do not judge your fellow until you have reached his place"—We can and often should condemn wrongdoing. But to judge the *person*, who he or she is inside, we are incapable of doing so unless we have "stood in his shoes." And doing that is simply impossible.

One may counter, "But I have had almost identical *nisyonos* (trials or temptations), and I never did what he did!" Perhaps, but a *nisayon* must be judged by the challenge it presents to the particular person, and every person is different. We would have pity (without condoning the act) on a destitute person who steals to relieve his hunger. But what of the many people who are emotionally destitute and who commit some transgression to still the hunger in their hearts? If you were not abused as a child, or if you had loving parents and a stable home, or if you did not grow up believing you were doomed to fail, you have no idea of the kind of inner torment and turmoil your neighbor (sometimes even your own spouse) might be living with.

I once knew a man who I found to be almost insufferably arrogant and rude, and I judged him harshly. When I met his brother and found him to be the same way, I realized that the character flaws were surely a product of their childhood—in some ways beyond their control.

When I was twenty, I had a job teaching Torah to six- and seven-year-old boys in a summer camp. I enjoyed the job, except for one child who seemed bent on making me and others miserable—all the more shocking because I knew what fine people his parents were. Decades later, I attended a meeting of Jews with alcohol and drug problems, at which this boy's brother (a man in his thirties) spoke. He mentioned how difficult his childhood had been, *having an alcoholic father* in a family that impressed upon him the need to keep the secret at all costs.

I wanted to go back in time to hug that little boy and beg forgiveness for my lack of compassion, which of course I could not. But it serves as a reminder: All adults were once little boys and girls, and how can we judge them when we do not really know them at all?

"And do not say something that cannot be heard (literally, that is impossible to be heard), for in the end it will be heard"—Rav Samson Raphael Hirsch explains this in a very beautiful way: If the world disregards the truth, do not say it is futile to speak because no one will listen. "Do not say it is impossible for your words to be heard, for in the end—tomorrow, or next year, or the year after that—it will be heard."

A different understanding, which (as I'll explain below) seems to better fit the rest of the Mishnah, is: "Do not tell others confidential information that you don't want repeated, for in the end it will be repeated and heard" by others. Or, as Benjamin Franklin put it: "Three can keep a secret only if two of them are dead." Even if your listener is a trustworthy person, people forget themselves and inadvertently slip up.

"And do not say, 'when I will be free, I will study,' for perhaps you will not be free"—"Regarding this, the minstrels say, 'Come to Cheshbon, let it be built and established as the city of Sichon'" (*Bamidbar* 21:27). King Sichon of Moav celebrated his conquests by planning a new capitol city to be called Cheshbon. Construction took time, effort, and money, but Cheshbon (picture "the Paris of the Middle East") was eventually completed. And shortly before the ribbon-cutting ceremony to inaugurate the capitol, Sichon went to attack the pesky Israelites, and he was defeated and killed. And when minstrels saw a man devoting all his energy to some project, ignoring all his todays for the sake of some far-off tomorrow, they would sing, "Remember Sichon and his city Cheshbon."

"Perhaps you will not be free" because of unforeseen circumstances, as Chazal put it, "*Harbeh kategorim mi'kan v'ad Gichon*—Many are the obstacles between here and the Gichon River." But aside from circumstance, we tend to assume that we will feel the same way tomorrow as we do today, which is often not the case.

Occasionally, someone asks for an appointment to meet with me to discuss how they can make progress in Torah learning or observance. If at all possible, I say, "How about meeting today or right now?" Enthusiasm dissipates, and today's interest becomes tomorrow's apathy without warning, and so we must strike while the iron is hot. (See Hillel's "If not now, when?" in Chapter 1, Mishnah 14.)

Is there a common theme to the Mishnah's five teachings? There is, and the theme is: We humans are more frail than we realize. "I don't need the community"; "I won't fall prey to temptation"; "I know enough to be able to judge my neighbor"; "I can trust my friend to keep a secret";

"I can put off serious learning or *tefillah* and get into it next month or next year." Like the most rare and exquisite flower, *kedushah* is as delicate as it beautiful, and as fragile as it is priceless.

ו. הוא היה אומר אין בור ירא חטא ולא עם הארץ חסיד ולא
הביישן למד ולא הקפדן מלמד ולא כל המרבה בסחורה מחכים
ובמקום שאין אנשים השתדל להיות איש.

Mishnah 6. He used to say: A boor cannot be sin-fearing; an am ha'aretz cannot be a chassid; the bashful cannot learn, and the overly strict cannot teach; and one excessively involved in business cannot become wise [in Torah]. And in a place where there are no men, strive to be a man.

An *am ha'aretz* is an unlearned Jew who was nevertheless raised to treat others with proper courtesy and respect (*derech eretz*), while a *boor* (similar to the English word boor) was raised by modern and progressive parents who believed in allowing the child to be his natural, savage, and dreadful self. As was true of most all Jews in ancient times, both *boor* and *am ha'aretz* were mitzvah observant.

It's a general rule that someone who does not act properly toward people around him will not act properly toward Hashem Whom he cannot see. Thus Chazal say that one who is ungrateful to other people will be ungrateful to Hashem, and Hashem says of children who mistreat their parents: "It is well that I did not live among them, for they would mistreat Me as well." A well-bred child learns rules and boundaries and the need for caution in word and deed, which helps prepare him for a life of *yiras Shamayim*. The *boor*, unaccustomed to boundaries and following his whims without regard to others, will keep whatever mitzvos he is used to but will not be sensitive to anything more.

The *am ha'aretz*, a "simple but pious Jew" who is devoted to serving Hashem and being helpful to other people, can be a *tzaddik*, but without a strong foundation of Torah learning (*Mesillas Yesharim* would add, "and a good measure of wisdom"), he does not have the knowledge to rise to higher spiritual levels. For instance, although many people like to make fun of *chumros* (stringencies in practical halachah), adopting the right *chumros* at the right time is part of the life of a *ben Torah*. But which ones are right for the particular individual, and when? Such as:

- When may someone be more *machmir* than his *rebbi*? Or the *rav* of the shul he is visiting?
- When may a married man take on a *chumrah* that will inconvenience his wife? This question has no simple one-size-fits-all answer.
- What if his *chumrah* makes his friends uncomfortable in his presence, or they make fun of him?
- When does the prohibition of *mechezei k'yuhara* (an appearance of arrogance) apply, not to mention actual *yuhara*, not just the appearance of it? Rav Dessler wrote that adopting even one relatively minor *chumrah* may lead a person to feel superior to all his friends and to serve as an excuse to neglect even important mitzvah obligations.

"And in a place where there are no men, strive to be a man"—"Man" in this context can mean a leader. If a certain community project needs doing and no one else will take it on, consider volunteering for it, even if others are more qualified. It is said that the Chafetz Chaim wanted others to write the *Mishnah Berurah*, but when he saw that no one else would do it, he made the project his own.

"Strive to be a man" can also include taking more responsibility for one's own Torah commitment ("to become a *gavra*," as we said in yeshiva), because the community's standards are too low to go along with the crowd. A certain young yeshiva man was a disappointment to his *rebbeim*, but when he married and moved to a small out-of-town community, he saw that he would not remain *frum* unless he changed his spiritually laid-back lifestyle, and he ended up being his town's pillar of Yiddishkeit and a *kanai* (zealot).

The Torah says that Noach was "perfect in his generation," and one opinion in Chazal is that since he was perfect in his wicked generation, how much more would he have achieved had he lived in the more righteous generation of Avraham Avinu. A second opinion is that Noach was perfect only in *his* generation, but had he lived in Avraham's time he would have been a nobody. The Alter from Novardok suggested that all agree on Noach's greatness, and the Sages differ only regarding Noach's *motivation*:

- One opinion is that Noach sought truth and spiritual advancement. Had he benefited from friends and mentors like Avraham, he would been even greater.

- The other opinion is that Noach would have been satisfied to be an ordinary middle-of-the-road *frum* person, but with society's negative influence all around him, he had no choice but to reach for the stars in order not to drown in the swamp. Had he been in Avraham Avinu's *beis midrash*, he would have been satisfied to sit in the back row, but living when he did, Noach had no choice but to "strive to be a man" of achievement.

ז. אַף הוּא רָאָה גֻּלְגֹּלֶת אַחַת שֶׁצָּפָה עַל פְּנֵי הַמַּיִם אָמַר לָהּ עַל דְּאַטֵּפְתְּ אַטְפוּךְ וְסוֹף מְטִיפַיִךְ יְטוּפוּן.

Mishnah 7. He also saw a skull that was floating on the water. He said to it: "Because you drowned others, they drowned you. And in the end, those who drowned you will be drowned."

Hashem had told Avraham that his descendants would be enslaved, so Pharaoh and the Egyptians who enslaved our ancestors were in a sense carrying out the Divine will. But since they were not commanded to do this evil but acted out of their own free will, they were held fully responsible for their crimes.

So too, when anyone does us any sort of harm, Hashem wanted it to happen, and we do deserve it (for reasons we may or may not be able to discern). But the one who does us harm has no excuse and is judged accordingly.

Hillel may have recognized the skull as that of a murderer who drowned others and had now received his just desserts. Or he may simply have meant: "You surely deserved this fate for some reason, but those who did it to you will be punished nonetheless."

It is worth noting that Hillel *spoke* to the skull. Expressing a truth
he already knew, he used the opportunity to be inspired and bring the
truth home to himself with powerful emotional force—seeing a decap-
itated murder victim makes an impact not soon forgotten. It's a lesson
for us to seize other such opportunities (they can be happy ones too!)
when they arise.

ט. רבן יוחנן בן זכאי קבל מהלל ומשמאי הוא היה אומר אם
למדת תורה הרבה אל תחזיק טובה לעצמך כי לכך נוצרת.

*Mishnah 9. Rabban Yochanan ben Zakkai received from Hillel
and Shammai. He used to say: If you learned much Torah, do
not give yourself credit, for this is what you were created to do.*

If anyone could be tempted to give himself some well-deserved
credit, it would be Rabban Yochanan ben Zakai, the outstanding *talmid
chacham* after the destruction of Yerushalayim and the Torah leader
who successfully negotiated with the Romans to ensure the continued
existence of the Sanhedrin and its sages. But Rabban Yochanan could
say to himself and to us, "Do not give yourself credit," for two reasons:

1. Studying Torah to the best of one's ability is an *obligation*, so
   how can you pat yourself on the back just for doing what you are
   obligated to do?

   However, I believe this reason can be challenged: Granted that all
   Jewish men are obligated to learn, but if I do more than everyone
   else to fulfill the obligation that we all share, then don't I have
   reason to feel proud and give myself credit?

2. However much I may have done, the lion's share of all I have
   accomplished was a special gift Hashem gave me for reasons
   known only to Him. "This (achievement) is what *you* alone were
   created to do." For instance, if I was born with a higher IQ than
   my neighbor, or if I was raised in a more Torah-oriented or more
   encouraging or more joyful family than my neighbor, or if I was
   granted more or better opportunities for Torah growth, can
   I give myself credit if I end up accomplishing more? And even

if I had the same or fewer opportunities, some people are born with more natural energy, diligence, or persistence than their neighbors. Since we have no way of knowing how much of our superiority is due to our own free will, how can we give ourselves credit? A taller person can reach higher, but he has done nothing to justify boasting about it.

י–יא. חמשה תלמידים היו לו לרבן יוחנן...הוא היה מונה שבחן. רבי אליעזר...בור סוד שאינה מאבד טפה. רבי יהושע...אשרי יולדתו. רבי יוסי...חסיד. רבי שמעון...ירא חטא. רבי אלעזר...כמעין המתגבר.

Mishnah 10–11. Rabban Yochanan ben Zakkai had five disciples...he used to enumerate their praises: Rabbi Eliezer...is a cemented cistern that loses not a drop. Rabbi Yehoshua...happy is she who gave birth to him. Rabbi Yosi...is a chassid. Rabbi Shimon...fears sin. Rabbi Elazar...is like a spring flowing ever stronger.

Why enumerate praises? One reason is, as Rav Yerucham Levovitz said: "Woe to the man who does not know his faults, for he does not know what he must correct. But double woe to the man who does not know his good points, for he does not know what tools he has with which to work."

We deceive ourselves and are largely unaware of our character flaws. But surprisingly, most of us don't really know our spiritual strengths either, at least not enough to identify the core good *middah* (character trait) that can serve as the foundation for a solid spiritual structure. We need another person, like a perceptive *rebbi* (*Sefer Cheshbon Ha'nefesh* suggests a perceptive parent) to evaluate us and "enumerate our praises."

"A cemented cistern" might mean the gift of a photographic memory, unconnected to character or piety, which would make this praise qualitatively different from "*chassid*" or one who "fears sin." But picture the young man who meets the girl of his dreams and asks for her telephone number. He does not have a pen (or cell phone!) to write it down, but if she dictates it to him, he remembers it. Because he views this piece of information as vital to his existence, it therefore sticks in his mind. Rabbi Eliezer saw every Torah lesson that way, and because of it he remembered them all.

"Happy is she who gave birth to him," because his mother receives *nachas* from other women's compliments about her son's sterling character. Chazal record a number of stories illustrating Rabbi Yehoshua's character—from his forbearance and willingness to be subservient to the Nasi Rabban Gamliel (who was not as great a *talmid chacham*), to his moral courage in standing firm in his halachic ruling, even in the face of an opposing *bas kol*.

"Like a spring flowing every stronger" means to be *"motzi davar mi'toch davar,"* analyzing the information and deriving new insights, applications, and general principles from it.

Like the "cemented cistern," this too might be only an intellectual rather than a moral quality, but not necessarily. If someone who learns Torah truly wants to be able to apply what he learns, then he will constantly ask himself, "What principle is being stated here? To what other cases might this principle be applied? What will be the halachah in another case that is almost identical except for one or more details, and what factors might affect the final *p'sak*?" A burning desire to know all that the page or paragraph is telling him is a powerful engine generating an endless number of new insights, "like a spring flowing ever stronger."

יב. הוא היה אומר אם יהיו כל חכמי ישראל בכף מאזנים ורבי אליעזר בן הורקנוס בכף שניה מכריע את כלם. אבא שאול אומר משמו אם יהיו כל חכמי ישראל בכף מאזנים ורבי אליעזר בן הוקרנוס אף עמהם ורבי אלעזר בן ערך בכף שניה מכריע את כלם.

Mishnah 12. He used to say: If all the Sages of Israel were on one pan of a balance-scale, and Eliezer ben Hurkenus in the other pan, he would outweigh them all. Abba Shaul said in his name: If all the Sages of Israel were on one pan of a balance-scale and even Rabbi Eliezer ben Hurkenus was with them, and Rabbi Elazar ben Arach was in the other pan, he would outweigh them all.

It is an astonishing statement to say that Rabbi Eliezer ben Hurkenus would outweigh all the other Sages put together, and even more astonishing to say that Rabbi Elazar ben Arach would outweigh all the Sages *including* Rabbi Eliezer ben Hurkenus. But what is this coming to teach us? Why record this in *Pirkei Avos*?

Besides their greatness, Rabbi Eliezer and Rabbi Elazar had something else in common: Both ended up isolated from the community of Torah Sages. When Rabbi Eliezer refused to accept the ruling of the majority in the matter of the *tanur shel achnai* (*Bava Metzia* 59a), he was excommunicated and remained so until his death. After Rabbi Elazar ben Arach left the Sages of Yavneh and moved to his wife's town, he gradually forgot his learning (although he later regained it) (*Shabbos* 147b), and is mentioned only a few times in the Gemara. Perhaps the lesson is that the most intellectually brilliant do not necessarily become the Torah leaders, and even genius comes with its own set of challenges.

יג. אמר להם צאו וראו איזו היא דרך טובה שידבק בה האדם.

Mishnah 13. He said to them: Go out and see which is the good path to which a person should attach himself.

See Mishnah 1 (above in this chapter) for a discussion of choosing a *derech* (path). Rabbi Yochanan does not tell his disciples what *derech* they should choose, even (as we will see) when he expresses his own preference for a particular *derech*. Each person is different and must seek the *derech* that works best for him—and the operative word is *seek*: "Go out and see" through trial and error and exploring alternatives to find your personal *derech*.

רבי אליעזר אומר: עין טובה.

Rabbi Eliezer says: A good eye.

To develop the habit of looking with a kindly eye at other people, and looking for the good in every situation, is not only a good *middah* but a comprehensive *derech* for life.

- A person with "a good eye" is a happier person, and is not likely to be resentful or complaining.
- He will avoid *lashon hara* and find it easier to fulfill the mitzvah of being *dan l'kaf zechus.*
- He will see the good, appreciate, and feel grateful for the myriad of kindnesses Hashem does for him continually—a huge step to attaining a living *emunah.*
- He will respond to misfortunes large and small with *"gam zu l'tovah"* (and mean it!), and go a long way toward developing true *bitachon.*

רבי יהושע אומר: חבר טוב.

Rabbi Yehoshua says: A good friend.

Some explain this to mean finding and keeping a good friend, a good Torah-devoted person who cares about you and in whom you can confide. To have someone you can tell anything to without fear of censure, who will advise and encourage and offer constructive criticism, who will point out when you are wrong and self-deluding, who will admire you for your good points, and who will offer sincere praise and much-needed hope is a treasure that most people never find.

However, valuable as a good friend is, the word *derech* would seem to imply something more comprehensive, like a life-plan or at least an attitude such as "a good eye" (but see what the *Rambam* writes in his Commentary on Mishnah about the far-ranging value of a friend). It would therefore be easier to explain this *derech* to mean to try to *be* a good friend to as many people as possible.

Here's a tip to help us work on this: Picture one of your acquaintances whom you don't dislike but are not particularly close to. His life seems to be going OK as far as you know. Now imagine that you read in his diary: "My bones shudder. My soul is utterly confounded...I am wearied with my sigh, every night I drench my bed with tears. My eye is dimmed because of anger, aged by my tormentors." Besides your surprise at his poetic writing style, wouldn't you feel a wave of compassion for this tormented soul whose sufferings you were totally unaware of?

The above-quoted words are of course from the daily *Tachanun*. But since Chazal told all of us to say these words, it means that deep inside every Jew, there is at least one part of him or her in which these words of suffering are true. Look again at your friend and ask yourself, "What terrible burden of anguish might he have? What inner demons might torment him, demons of whose existence I am completely unaware?" Medical, financial, familial, emotional, spiritual problems—any congregational rabbi can tell you that there are very many whose suffering is unknown to everyone around them.

Look again at your neighbor, bring out your compassion, and say: "I can't take away his pain (especially since I don't know what it is), but I can add a small measure of joy and comfort to his life by trying to be his friend." After focusing on one acquaintance, move on to another, and little by little your circle of love begins to grow and you become transformed.

רבי יוסי אומר: שכן טוב.

Rabbi Yosi says: A good neighbor.

As the *Rambam* writes (and as we have noted more than once) in *Hilchos De'os*, human nature is that we imitate our neighbors' attitudes and action, and Rabbi Yosi might be saying that surrounding ourselves with the best possible neighbors is a *derech* that pays huge dividends for a very small investment of effort (as in the case of my friend from Freehold in Mishnah 5).

Selecting the "best" neighborhood sometimes requires careful study, and each family has different needs. *Baalei teshuvah, geirei tzedek,* or out-of-the-box types sometimes (I stress, only *sometimes*) don't fit well in more *yeshivish* communities, and small-town dwellers who move to a Torah metropolis sometimes end up never finding a *rav* to help guide them.

Even among seasoned *b'nei Torah*, I know a *kollel* family of modest means who live very simply—like most *kollel* families did a generation or two ago. The wife told me that if they lived in Lakewood, New Jersey, a magnificent Torah community but one in which many *kollel* families have a much higher standard of living, the pressure to do likewise (especially in providing for their children) might make it impossible for her husband to remain in *kollel*.

But another way to understand this Mishnah, a way that I think fits better with the word *"derech,"* is not so much to have a good neighbor as to *be* a good neighbor to all our neighbors. Whereas Rabbi Yehoshua's *derech* of being a good friend focuses on developing love for another, Rabbi Yosi focuses more on developing a pattern of helpfulness, honesty, and concern for people we might not choose as friends. For instance:

- Showing a cheerful willingness to lend a tool or lend a hand
- Shoveling snow off your sidewalk (or even your neighbor's sidewalk!), and taking extra care not to injure a neighbor's property or deprive him of his sleep or his parking space
- Keeping your front lawn (and the sidewalk) uncluttered with toys, obstacles, or eyesores
- Extending a smile and a hearty greeting as you pass by, with an occasional compliment ("you have a beautiful baby/garden/dog") when warranted
- Giving neighbors help (without being asked) in times of celebration or sadness. And not just asking, "What can I do?" but finding what needs doing and doing it

The Alter from Slabodka taught that saying "Good morning" is actually giving the other person a blessing (i.e., "May Hashem give you a good morning"), and when he walked past the homes of *b'nei Torah*, he would sometimes say "Good morning," even though the residents could not hear him. Since the Torah says that Hashem blesses those who bless Jews, this is an easy way to get lots of *berachos* for yourself.

This is a comprehensive *derech* that helps develop *chessed*, empathy, and discernment—to be on the lookout for ways to help or mistakes to avoid, and we can put it to use with almost everyone we meet.

רבי שמעון אומר: הרואה את הנולד.

Rabbi Shimon says: One who foresees what will occur.

This is a comprehensive *derech*, because it encompasses a pattern of thinking to be followed throughout the day, and it is a skill that develops with use. For example:

- When I see my friend Shmeryl today, I know from experience that he is likely to (choose as many as apply): a. bad-mouth someone; b. complain about something; c. criticize me; d. lament his troubles, real or imagined; e. try to detain me long after I wish to leave. Since I expect it to happen, let me plan now how I will respond when it does.

- Friends are going to ask my opinion about: (a) the *machlokes* in the shul; (b) the national political situation; (c) Shmeryl's impending divorce. Let me plan now how I will respond.

- Experience shows that certain conversation topics upset or enrage my brother-in-law. At our next visit, what can I do to avoid those topics, and what should I do if someone else brings them up?

- When I meet with my client this afternoon, what issues is he likely to bring up, and what do I plan to say about them?

- At the shul *kiddush* this Shabbos, I will be sorely tempted to break my diet. How do I plan to avoid that happening? (Leave immediately after saying *"mazel tov,"* eat only what my spouse puts on my plate, or avoid the cake by stuffing myself with herring, etc.)

- I know at *Minchah* I'll be distracted by thoughts of tomorrow's deal. How do I plan to have *kavanah* for at least a paragraph or two?

- My first marriage ended in divorce, and I am at least partly to blame. What stresses are likely to appear in my upcoming second marriage, and how will I deal with them?

- I will die one day and be judged. Let me try to visualize my appearance before the Heavenly Court ("foresee what will occur"): What might the Court say, and what can I do now before it's too late to modify the verdict in my favor?

רבי אלעזר אומר: לב טוב.

Rabbi Elazar says: A good heart.

Rav Avigdor Miller pointed out that in Tanach, the word "heart" means "*mind*." But "a good mind" is so general a statement that it is difficult to know what *derech* it might refer to.

I once saw a suggestion that the good-heart *derech* means a program of developing the "ought" muscle. Typical temptations involve a struggle between "I ought" and "I want": "I ought to get up, but I want to sleep more"; "I ought to remain silent, but I want to gossip"; "I ought to close the refrigerator, but I want the cake" and so on. The old *mussar-niks* used to practice overcoming desire in little things, several times a day (like eating only half the dessert, waiting a day to open mail, delaying angry words until pulling a special jacket from the closet). The habit of having the will trump desire strengthens our willpower, or the "ought" muscle, to gradually be able to take on larger and more difficult challenges and win.

אמר להם רואה אני את דברי אלעזר בן ערך מדבריכם שבכלל
דבריו דבריכם.

He [Rabban Yochanan] said to them: I see [prefer] the words of Elazar ben Arach to your words, for included in his words are your words.

Rabban Yochanan seems to say that we should choose the *derech* of "a good heart," but if that is his intent, there is a problem. In the very next Mishnah, he tells his disciples to go out and see what is the "evil path" from which to distance oneself. All except Rabbi Shimon conclude that the evil path is the opposite of the good path, and Rabban Yochanan unsurprisingly prefers Rabbi Elazar's choice of an "evil heart." But didn't the other disciples realize that their *rebbi* would again say that Rabbi Elazar's *derech* (of what to avoid) was best? And since they must have realized it, why did they stick with their previous choices?

The answer is that even the "best" (i.e., most productive) *derech* is not best for everyone. Trying to be a Brisker does not work for every yeshiva man, and not everyone is cut out to be a chassid or a *mussar-nik*. After hearing Rabbi Yochanan's praise of the "good heart," his *talmidim* understood that he would single out the "evil heart" as the most important *derech* to avoid, but that did not affect their conclusions as to what their answers should be for themselves.

יד. רבי שמעון אומר הלוה ואינו משלם אחד הלוה מן האדם
כלוה מן המקום...

Mishnah 14. Rabbi Shimon says: One who borrows and does not repay—it is the same whether one borrows from another person or from G-d [HaMakom]...

All the *talmidim* concluded that the "evil path" was the opposite of the good one, except for Rabbi Shimon. Is there some way in which "one who foresees what will occur" and "one who borrows but does not repay" are opposites?

All our blessings—life, eyesight, hearing, arms and legs, family, friends, food (the list is endless)—are Hashem's gifts to us, but they are actually loans given to us for a limited number of years and intended to be used in accordance with His Will (our "repayment"). If we do not do so, it is usually because we find it hard to picture that there will indeed be a day of reckoning after 120 years—to "foresee what will occur."

Our relationships with other people, whom we can see, are in many ways training for relating to Hashem, Whom we cannot see. Being in the habit of promptly repaying every debt, including debts of gratitude, engenders feelings of responsibility to help us feel that Hashem's "loans" must also be repaid and to act promptly before they fall due.

The Name "*HaMakom*" is used because it signifies Hashem as "*Mekomo shel Olam*—The Place (the One Who holds up) the world." All that we possess, and all reality, is only from Him continually sustaining it all.

טו. הם אמרו שלשה דברים:

Mishnah 15. They said three things:

They taught thousands of lessons, but they repeated these three continually. If too many lessons are stressed as "the most important," none
of them are absorbed as such. Perhaps three is the maximum number to
present as core teachings. (It is also good advice for public speakers not
to make more than three points in a single lecture.)

רבי אליעזר אומר: יהי כבוד חברך חביב עליך כשלך ואל תהי
נוח לכעוס.

*Rabbi Eliezer says: Let the honor of your friend be as dear to
you as your own, and do not be easily angered.*

Rabbi Eliezer is teaching us how to avoid becoming angry. When I am
upset with someone, I tend to lash out, thinking of my own emotional
pain without considering (or realizing) how much damage my outburst
might cause. If I would realize that my angry words might remain in my
neighbor's memory for decades (as so often occurs), and that every time
they come to mind it will reinforce in him feelings of low self-esteem, year
after year, I would not show anger. If other people are also present, the
pain of dishonor to my neighbor is multiplied, and picturing the damage
I would cause will go a long way toward getting myself under control.

ושוב יום אחד לפני מיתתך.

And repent one day before your death.

And since we truly do not know that we will live through tomorrow,
surely we must repent today. This is strong medicine, but for most of
us it is very difficult to picture death and live accordingly day after day.
But there is another application of this principle that is easier (and less
depressing) to use.

Koheles tells us: "At all times let your garments be white" in celebration. But Chazal say that the "white garments" mean *shrouds*, to always
be prepared for the day of death, which is somewhat odd. A Midrash
generally adds depth to the plain meaning of the *pasuk*, yet here, it
seems to teach the very opposite of the plain meaning!

Rav Isaac Sher explained that there is no contradiction. The *pasuk*
says to celebrate each day, and the Midrash shows us the way to feel

how precious each day is—by say to yourself: "*I will live this day as if it were my last.*"

If I had but one more day, I would make sure to tell my spouse and children how much I love them and what they mean to me. I would savor the sunlight, pour out my heart in my last davening, and feel my soul bond with one last hour of Torah learning. I would truly see, possibly for the first time, how much I have for which to thank Hashem—to see how beautiful life is, and how beautiful my friends and neighbors are, and to celebrate being surprised by joy. I will live this day as if it were my last, experience all the blessings Hashem gives me this special day, and immerse myself in each precious moment as no one else ever can.

והוי מתחמם כנגד אורן של חכמים והוי זהיר בגחלתן שלא תכוה...

And warm yourself by the fire of the Sages, but beware of their glowing coal so that you not be burned...

Besides learning Torah from the Sages, we should try to be in their company ("warm yourself by the fire") as much as possible to learn from their ordinary speech (*sichas chullin*) and actions. Rabbi Yehudah HaNasi's maidservant picked up much Torah wisdom (mentioned several times in the Gemara) without ever being in his yeshiva.

However, at the same time, we must beware that familiarity should not lead to a lessening of our reverence. The Kohen Gadol entered the Holy of Holies only once a year; going more often would diminish his sense of awe.

I will never forget the first time I saw Rav Moshe Feinstein and heard him speak. It was as if the air was filled with electricity, and I was riveted to my chair. But it was less so the second time I heard him, and the third time even less. He had not changed, but I had in some way become used to him. This is only natural and not completely unavoidable, but we must be on guard that the awe should not become less than it need be.

טז. רבי יהושע אומר עין הרע ויצר הרע ושנאת הבריות מוציאין
את האדם מן העולם.

Mishnah 16. Rabbi Yehoshua says: An evil eye, the yetzer hara,
and hatred of people take a person out from the world.

"The world" might refer to *Olam Haba* (the World to Come), but if so, it should say that these things prevent a person from entering there. "Take a person out" implies a taking out from where he or she already is, which is *this* world. These three things ruin the natural enjoyment of life by substituting in our minds an imaginary world for the real one. They "take us out" from reality to a place of darkness and gloom, and if we never truly live in this world, how can we hope to merit the World to Come?

- "An evil eye"—To be in the habit of seeing the bad in everything is to be always complaining and never feel grateful—a never-ending sadness.
- "*Yetzer Hara*" would seem to mean that power that tempts us to any sin, but without a *yetzer hara*, we would probably not be afflicted with an evil eye or hatred of other people either. In this Mishnah, the term probably means something more specific. *Yetzer hara* is often used to refer to lust, especially sexual desire, though Chazal say that *yetzer hara* is necessary even for *tzaddikim* to fully enjoy their Torah learning (compare Freud's *Eros*, a physical energy that can be sublimated toward higher ends). But a person who cannot control his lusts becomes controlled by them (sometimes recognized as addiction), ultimately abandoning the Torah and all the joys of life.
- "Hatred of people"—Just as *ahavas ha'beriyos* ("love of people") means a positive attitude toward people in general, so too "hatred of people" means a negative attitude toward the human race, with exceptions made for *his* family and *his* friends, whom he likes because they meet *his* needs. The book *Type-A Behavior and Your Heart* notes that many people walk around in a state of "free-flowing hostility," ready to select any available target for

their resentment. As one of the *mussar sefarim* put it, "The angry man wakes up angry, and looks for someone to be the object of his anger." Besides being far from righteousness, he is of course also very miserable.

יז. רבי יוסי אומר יהי ממון חברך חביב עליך כשלך והתקן עצמך ללמוד תורה שאינה ירושה לך וכל מעשיך יהיו לשם שמים.

Mishnah 17. Rabbi Yosi says: Let your fellow's money be as dear to you as your own. And prepare [hasken] yourself to study Torah, for it is not an inheritance to you. And let all your deeds be for the sake of Heaven.

"Let your fellow's money (the word *mammon* can also mean 'possessions') be as dear to you as your own" is a practical tip to help us become a good neighbor, which Rabbi Yosi encouraged as a *derech* in Mishnah 13. This goes beyond avoiding all dishonesty; if my neighbor's empty trash can lies in the gutter where it might be damaged, or a newspaper delivered to his home was placed where it might be lost, or anything of his was left out in the rain, I will go out of my way to help, imagining what I would do if the possessions were my own.

"Prepare yourself to study Torah"—Serious Torah study does not come naturally to some people, who may conclude that such study is simply not for them. But Torah study is for everyone, and indeed it does *not* come naturally. Inheritance comes naturally without *kinyan* (acts of acquisition), but Torah must be acquired by developing the habit of hard work, concentration, and persistence. Even when Torah study *does* come naturally, higher levels of achievement always demand training comparable to that of a world-class musician or athlete, including the forty-eight *kinyanim* listed in the Mishnah in Chapter 6.

"And let all your deeds be for the sake of Heaven"—This can be practiced on three levels, at least one of which is possible for everyone. To take the example of eating:

- The highest level: "I cannot stay alive and healthy to do Hashem's will unless I eat, so I will eat (only healthy foods, of course, and only in the amounts required to maintain good health). Otherwise, I would not eat at all."

- The intermediate level: "I eat because I enjoy eating, but I will choose those foods and in those amounts that a person at the highest level would choose, and will thereby be eating 'for the sake of Heaven' as well as my own enjoyment."

- The lower (and very attainable) level: "I eat because I enjoy eating, and many of my food choices are not what a holy person would choose. But whatever I eat that *is* healthful, since it keeps me alive and healthy to be able to do Hashem's will, I will add the *thought* that I am also 'eating for the sake of Heaven.'"

This is not false. Regardless of my motives, dinner does help me serve Hashem (even dessert, if it gives me a lift and encourages me to go to *Maariv* or a *shiur*). And adding the thought elevates the meal into a spiritual achievement. Rav Avigdor Miller actually taught that when sitting down at the table, one should say the words aloud: "I am eating *l'shem Shamayim.*" It's an easy mitzvah, and from his place in Heaven, Rabbi Yosi might well give you a blessing for it.

יח. רבי שמעון אומר הוי זהיר בקריאת שמע ובתפלה וכשאתה
מתפלל אל תעש תפלתך קבע אלא רחמים ותחנונים לפני
המקום...ואל תהי רשע בפני עצמך.

Mishnah 18. Rabbi Shimon says: Be careful in saying the Shema and prayer, and when you pray, do not make your prayer a fixed routine, but [a plea for] mercy and supplication before the Omnipresent...and do not be a wicked person within yourself.

Since Rabbi Shimon's *derech* to "foresee what will occur" includes imagining us someday standing before Hashem to be judged (see our notes to Mishnah 13), it fits well that he emphasizes exercising our imagination to see ourselves standing before Hashem every day.

"Do not be a wicked person within yourself"—This might be (though it does not need to be) connected to his previous statement; begging for mercy in prayer continually reminds us of our low state and the need for mercy because of our sins. It is therefore a danger to think: "Since I am a worthless sinner, what's the point of trying to improve?" There must be balance, as one *rebbi* said: "Keep two pieces of paper in your pockets, one of which reads 'I am dust and ashes,' and the other, 'For my sake the universe was created.' There are times when he should take out one slip, and times when he should take out the other."

"Do not be a wicked person within yourself"—Do not see yourself as wicked, but neither should you see yourself as a *tzaddik*. One approach might be what I heard from a *talmid* of Rav Aharon Kotler: "The Rosh Yeshiva made you feel that the whole future of Klal Yisrael rested on your shoulders," i.e., that you were given a great mission and were blessed with the talent and potential to do great things, which meant you also shouldered a great responsibility to aspire to nothing less than greatness itself.

יט. רבי אלעזר אומר הוי שקוד ללמוד תורה ודע מה שתשיב לאפיקורוס ודע לפני מי אתה עמל ומי הוא בעל מלאכתך שישלם לך שכר פעלתך.

Mishnah 19. Rabbi Elazar says: (1) Be diligent to study Torah; (2) and know what you will answer to an unbeliever [apikores]; (3) and know before Whom you toil, Who your Employer is, and Who will pay you the reward for your actions.

"Be diligent to study Torah"—Even if you are learning well, if you are not putting in all your effort (*shakud*), you are missing out. It is not only that more effort produces more and better results. It is that putting in our best efforts is part of "*ol Torah*," accepting the "yoke of Torah," a prerequisite for being a student in the yeshiva of Hakadosh Baruch Hu, "*Ha'melamed Torah l'amo Yisrael.*"

"And know what you will answer to an *apikores*"—Apikores can be a generic term for an unbeliever, or more specifically for a scoffer who mocks *talmidei chachamim* and their teachings. Some note that the Mishnah tells us to "know what to answer," but does not say we should actually engage in debate, which is bound to be unproductive and may do us harm. But we need to know for *ourselves* how to respond to argument and mockery: What is the solid ground on which we base our *emunah*? What is it that gives us the enormous pride to laugh at fools who would poke fun at us, no matter how numerous they may be?

"Who will pay you"—Ideally, we should serve Hashem *lishmah* (for its own sake), yet Chazal say that "a man should always engage in Torah study and mitzvos even not for their own sake." Rav Avraham Grodzensky of Slabodka noted the word "*always*" and thus taught this to mean that even the idealist should use the power of *lo lishmah* (self-interest) to give him an extra boost as needed.

Ideally, knowing that each word of Torah is worth millions should not be the reason I sit down to learn, but it might keep me by the *sefer* a little longer or be the deciding factor when I feel tempted to abandon the *sefer* altogether.

 כ. רבי טרפון אומר היום קצר והמלאכה מרבה והפועלים עצלים
והשכר הרבה ובעל הבית דוחק.

Mishnah 20. Rabbi Tarfon says: The day is short, the work is great, the workers are lazy, the reward is great, and the Employer is demanding [dochek].

"The day" refers to today—the one we are in right now. Instead of making excuses to put off serious Torah achievement to "down the road," realize that there is much to be done ("the work is plentiful") right now. First thing in the morning (or the night before), ask, "What do I hope to achieve today?" and do your best to follow through.

"The workers are lazy" is a fact I must accept about myself. Much of what I ought to do today seems difficult and not enjoyable, but rather than use that as an excuse ("I'm just not a *zariz*"), accept it as the rules of the game and slog on until you reach the finish line.

"The reward is great"—Chazal said that a mitzvah that is difficult (*tzaar*) is worth a hundred times the same act without difficulty. Based on this, the *baalei mussar* explained that a mitzvah with two degrees of difficulty is worth a hundred times the same act with one degree of difficulty, and three degrees of difficulty are worth another hundred times more than two. When I'm tired or ready to give up, pushing myself that extra little bit is priceless and helps to develop the persistence muscles that make it easier in the long run.

"The Employer is demanding"—Ultimately, whatever we can achieve is what we are meant to achieve, and I must not compare myself with others who do far less—only with the great success I am meant to become.

כא. הוא היה אומר לא עליך המלאבה לגמור...אם למדת תורה הרבה נותנים לך שכר הרבה. ונאמן הוא בעל מלאבתך שישלם לך שכר פעלתך.

Mishnah 21. He used to say: It is not upon you to complete the work...If you learned much Torah, you will be given much reward. And your Employer can be trusted that He will pay you the reward of your actions.

"It is not upon you to complete the work"—There is always more Torah to be learned and more perfection of deeds and character to be achieved, so it would seem that Rabbi Tarfon is teaching us only that which we already know (unless he only wishes to emphasize that we should not use the enormity of the task as an excuse to do little or nothing).

But "the work" also refers to important community mitzvah projects, which may not—and in some cases, cannot—be completed in your lifetime. Builders of Torah in the first decades of twentieth-century America had very limited success, but it was they who laid the foundations that made possible today's astounding Torah renaissance. In Vienna in 1915, Rabbi Flesch's lasting influence on his community may not have been great, but he inspired a visitor from Poland named Sarah Schenirer to revolutionize the Jewish world.

"If you learned much Torah, you will be given much reward"—At first glance, this statement seems self-evident and teaches nothing new, but contrast it with: "It is the same whether one does much or little, as long as one's heart is directed to Heaven."

Rav Avigdor Miller reportedly said that in Slabodka, he was taught that "there is an *Olam Haba* for effort, and another *Olam Haba* for achievement." I pray that my attempt to explain this is on the right track.

Picture two young men, Reuven and Shimon. Reuven has a brilliant mind, nurtured by his *talmid chacham* father and top-notch *rebbeim*, and he grows up to become a world-renowned Rosh Yeshiva with many hundreds of *talmidim*. Shimon is of average (or slightly below-average) intelligence, the son of sincere but unlearned parents who send him to the local day school. Shimon grows up to be a *frum* blue-collar worker who religiously attends a nightly *daf yomi shiur* after a long day's work, but more advanced learning is beyond him.

Assuming they put in the same amount of effort, it would seem that they would receive equal reward when they reach the Next World, and if Shimon put in more effort than Reuven, his reward would be even greater. And though in this world we revere Rav Reuven and thousands of us seek his words of *daas Torah* to guide and inspire us, at the same time, we are aware that in Hashem's eyes, there are (many) Shimons who are greater.

Do we truly believe this to be true?

And if indeed it is true that in *Olam Haba* only effort is important, consider Levi who lives in Eretz Yisrael and Yehudah who lives elsewhere and is unable to make *aliyah*. They serve Hashem with the same amount of effort, but only Levi fulfills the mitzvos of *terumos, maasros, sheviis* and *yishuv ha'aretz*. If (using the effort yardstick) they will receive equal reward, are we not implying that all the additional mitzvos of Eretz Israel have no effect, Heaven forbid?

It seems that we must conclude that, essential as effort is, the achievement of learning more Torah and fulfilling more mitzvos is also important ("another *Olam Haba* for achievement"). If this is so, Rabbi Tarfon is indeed teaching us something radically new: "More Torah = more reward" because achievement itself brings reward, even if the path to success was aided by intellectual gifts and a nurturing environment.

Why this should be so, i.e., why Shimon would put in as much effort as Reuven and yet receive less reward, I do not know. One possibility is as Rav Avigdor Miller said, referring to the Avos, that "Hashem knows beforehand who will choose greatness," and Reuven was given gifts because Hashem knew he would use them. But this implies that such gifts were withheld from hard-working Shimon because Hashem knew Shimon would not make use of them, and therefore anyone who is not intellectually gifted should know that he would not have worked hard enough to become a *talmid chacham*, even if he had the IQ. Many (including myself) find this to be an unsatisfactory answer.

(To end this discussion with something I heard from Rav Miller in response to a different question, "For an answer to that question, you'll have to ask me when I'm older.")

Chapter Three

א. עקביא בן מהללאל אומר הסתכל בשלשה דברים ואין אתה
בא לידי עברה. דע מאין באת ולאן אתה הולך ולפני מי אתה
עתיד לתן דין וחשבון. מאין באת מטפה סרוחה ולאן אתה הולך
למקום עפר רמה ותולעה. ולפני מי אתה עתיד לתן דין וחשבון
לפני מלך מלכי המלכים הקדוש ברוך הוא.

Mishnah 1. Akavia ben Mahallalel says: Look carefully at three things and you will not come to the hands of sin. Know whence you came—a putrid drop. And where you are going—to a place of dirt, maggots and worms,. And before Whom you are destined to stand for judgment and an accounting—before the King of Kings, the Holy One, blessed be He.

The first Mishnah in Chapter 2 also taught to look carefully at three things, but they are not the same three. One can suggest that the two Mishnayos refer to different circumstances, but since the wording is identical ("Look carefully at three things, and you will not come to the hands of sin"), it is more likely that the two Mishnayos complement one another. The Mishnah in Chapter 2 focuses on thinking about Hashem Who sees, hears, and records our deeds. Akavia ben Mahallalel focuses on how we should think about ourselves: "Whence *you* came, and where *you* are going, and before Whom *you* are destined to stand in judgment."

"Whence you came"—Most great temptations are in the category of *gaavah* (arrogance, anger, status-seeking) or *taavah* (desires of the flesh). Remembering that we come from nothing gives us perspective that can help us avoid *gaavah* (though not totally, e.g., Winston Churchill reportedly said that "we are all worms, but I do believe that I am a glow-worm").

"And where you are going"—Some explain that thoughts of the grave dampen physical desires, though I don't know that this is true for most people. But a friend told me that the day he received a diagnosis of cancer, all his desires suddenly seemed petty and unappealing. Thinking about one's own death can be strong medicine to be taken only occasionally (to avoid side effects), but awareness that our condition is terminal and the termination date is unknown to us can have a sobering effect.

"And before Whom you are destined to stand for judgment and an accounting"—Some explain that "accounting" refers to potential; an upstanding lay leader of the *frum* community who could have become a true *Gadol B'Torah* had he put in the effort is judged not only according to his deeds but also in comparison to the Jew he could have become.

"Before the King of Kings"—If we were to be judged by Hashem's designated Heavenly Court of angels or *tzaddikim*, would that make any difference? Perhaps the Mishnah is hinting at something I once heard regarding whether a bit of dishonesty was permitted in a certain financial matter: "Even if you think it's *mutar* (permitted), do you think it's what Hakadosh Baruch Hu wants?"

We tend to categorize our actions as Divinely commanded, Divinely prohibited, and *pareve* (neutral). But the *Chovos Halevavos* teaches that since ultimately every action either draws us toward or leads us away from Hashem, no act is neutral.

I was once asked to say a few words to a Christian group at an assembly to be held in a church, and after weighing the halachic pros and cons, I concluded that it was halachically permitted in that particular case. But since "permitted" does not necessarily mean "recommended," in the end I asked myself: "If I did not speak at the church, then when I someday appear before the King of Kings, do I think He will be upset with me for not having spoken there?" That decided the issue for me.

ב. רבי חנינא סגן הכהנים אומר הוי מתפלל בשלומה של מלכות
שאלמלא מוראה איש את רעהו חיים בלעו.

*Mishnah 2. Rabbi Chanina, the second-in-command [s'gan] of
the Kohanim, says: Pray for the welfare of the government, for
if not for fear of it, man would swallow his fellow man alive.*

This appears to be a straightforward halachah—that we should pray for
the government, even an oppressive government like that of the Romans
(under whom Rabbi Chanina lived), because the alternatives of anarchy
and lawlessness are worse. If so, it is different from most Mishnayos in
Avos. But Rabbi Chanina is coming to teach us more than a halachah.

It seems that he does *not* mean merely that anarchy would allow
criminals to roam free, but that even good people ("*ish es rei'eihu*) could
descend into barbarism. As Hillel warned (Chapter 2, Mishnah 5), "Do
not believe in (i.e., trust) yourself until the day you die," because it is
possible for even the finest person to fall into depravity.

In addition, we learn here that all of us need the extra boost from
external supports. I exercise my free will to refrain from shoplifting,
but my moral choice is made easier by the knowledge that getting
caught will have ruinous consequences. I respond to a request for help
because I know it is the right thing to do, but knowing that refusing to
help will make me look bad encourages me to do what I know I should.
The *Chovos Halevavos* goes so far as to say that without fear of shame,
people would neither help others nor honor their parents.

This does not mean that we are hypocrites, but that our weak wills
need all the help they can get. That's why telling your New Year's resolution to all your friends ("I'm going to learn *daf yomi*; lose ten pounds;
daven with a minyan" etc.) helps ensure that you'll keep it; your *yetzer
tov* overcomes the *yetzer hara* of laziness by enlisting the assistance of
the *yetzer hara* of *kavod*.

ג. רבי חנינא בן תרדיון אומר שנים שיושבין ואין ביניהם דברי
תורה הרי זה מושב לצים שנאמר ובמושב לצים לא ישב. אבל
שנים שיושבין ויש ביניהם דברי תורה שכינה שרויה ביניהם.

Mishnah 3. Rabbi Chanina ben Teradyon says: If two sit together and there are no words of Torah between them, this is an assembly of scoffers, as it is said [Tehillim 1:1]: "And in the assembly of scoffers he did not sit." But if two sit together and there are words of Torah between them, the Divine Presence [Shechinah] rests with them.

How does the *pasuk* tell us that two people sitting together without speaking words of Torah are an "assembly of scoffers"? The Mishnah derives it from the *pasuk* taken in context: "Fortunate is the man who did not walk in the counsel of the wicked…and in the assembly of scoffers he did not sit. But in the Torah of Hashem is his desire, and in His Torah he speaks day and night." The *pasuk* implies that there are only two choices: speaking in Hashem's Torah or being part of the assembly of scoffers.

Two people who meet to work on a community project, or even to discuss personal work-related issues, are obviously not considered "scoffers." But the Mishnah is teaching that in conversations without Torah, the conversation's *natural tendency* is to end up badmouthing other people or institutions, or to try to assert one's superiority over the other fellow. The reason for this is the ego's never-ending desire to rise above others, and putting others down is often the easiest way to do so. Torah study requires us to subordinate the ego to the search for Hashem's truth, ennobling the entire conversation.

ד. רבי שמעון אומר שלשה שאכלו על שלחן אחד ולא אמרו עליו דברי תורה כאלו אכלו מזבחי מתים שנאמר כי כל שלחנות מלאו קיא צואה בלי מקום.

Mishnah 4. Rabbi Shimon says: If three ate at one table [i.e., they ate together] and they did not speak words of Torah, it is as if they ate from offerings to the dead [idols], as it is said [Yeshayah 28:8]: "For all tables are full of vomit and filth, without makom."

The plain meaning of the *pasuk* is to denounce the idol-worshippers whose tables are all full of idolatrous sacrifices that are like vomit and filth (*Rashi*) without a clean place (*Radak*). But the concluding words "*bli makom*" literally mean "without a place," and the word "clean" is not mentioned. Rabbi Shimon therefore takes the word "*Makom*" to mean "the Omnipresent" (Hashem), and the *pasuk* now reads: "For all their tables are full of idolatrous sacrifices, *because their meal* is without *mention of* the Omnipresent."

Like in Mishnah 3, we are told that there are only two choices, but idol-worship is surely worse than general scoffing. What wrong is committed here that is greater than that of Mishnah 2?

The Gemara says: "*Gadol legimah*—Great is the power of giving (food and) drink." When people eat together, their inhibitions break down and they begin to bond, which is why a business lunch is so often the setting for business negotiations. But the breaking down of inhibitions, especially if helped along by wine (as was the practice in meals in Talmudic times) loosens moral restraints. Even if nothing bad happens, the meal tends to be a step in the wrong direction, which is why the Gemara says a *talmid chacham* would not eat a meal unless he knew who the others guests would be.

Rav Yehudah Jacobs of Lakewood told me that the Rosh Yeshiva, Rav Aharon Kotler, thought long and hard before deciding to include a dining room in the yeshiva. A young Torah scholar eating in his room or with a family maintains his dignity, while the atmosphere in a student dining-hall can degenerate to that of a high-school cafeteria, complete with food fights and throwing pieces of kugel...

אבל שלשה שאכלו על שלחן אחד ואמרו עליו דברי תורה כאלו
אכלו משלחנו של מקום.

But if three ate at one table and spoke words of Torah, it is as if they ate from the table of the Omnipresent.

Precisely because of the natural tendency of inhibitions to break down at a communal meal, those who fight the tendency by elevating their gathering with words of Torah are accomplishing something out of the ordinary, and Hashem considers them guests at a dinner table of His own.

ה. רבי חנינא בן חכינאי אומר הנעור בלילה והמהלך בדרך יחידי
ומפנה לבו לבטלה הרי זה מתחייב בנפשו.

*Mishnah 5. Rabbi Chanina ben Chachinai says: Someone who
is awake at night, or who walks alone on the road, and turns
his heart (mind) to idle thoughts, has sinned against his soul
[or: has forfeited his life].*

If the sin here is *bitul Torah*, it would not be confined to nighttime or
travel. Instead, it refers to thinking about the great questions of life we
must ask ourselves, but seldom do: "*Why am I here in this world? What
will happen to me when I die? What does Hashem want of me? What should
I change, and how should I go about it?*" Solitude gives us the opportunity
to think about these things, and more importantly, to meditate, to turn
the ideas over and over in our minds, and to try to internalize them as
realities. Most people will not take the trouble to set aside times for
serious thought, but when an effortless opportunity presents itself,
e.g., alone on the road or late at night, to ignore it is truly a sin against
one's own soul.

ו. רבי נחוניא בן הקנה אומר כל המקבל עליו עול תורה מעבירין
ממנו עול מלכות ועול דרך ארץ וכל הפורק ממנו עול תורה
נותנין עליו עול מלכות ועול דרך ארץ.

*Mishnah 6. Rabbi Nechunia ben Hakaneh says: Whoever
accepts upon himself the yoke of Torah, the yoke of government
and the yoke of making a living [and other social responsibilities]
[derech eretz] are removed from him. And whoever throws off
from himself the yoke of Torah, the yoke of government and
derech eretz is placed upon him.*

Some understand this "removal of the yoke" as special Divine assistance to free the Torah person from other responsibilities. One who
"throws off the yoke of Torah" is given other burdens—not necessarily
as punishment, but because human beings with too much leisure time
inevitably get into trouble.

But we can also understand this in a natural way as referring to an emotional yoke: Too many people are obsessed with keeping up with the news and worrying about it, especially various kinds of political news (the yoke of government). And how much energy do we expend worrying about our finances and our careers (the yoke of *derech eretz*)?

The Jew who has voluntarily accepted the yoke of Torah is not oblivious to current events, and he also puts in the necessary effort to make a living, but his emotional energy is not drained away with worry, because the focus of his day is elsewhere. If I have a magnificent obsession to learn and review a certain number of *blatt Gemara* this year, and each day I awaken thinking about this day's goal, I give other concerns their due, but not more than their due.

In the midst of World War II, Winston Churchill said, "I have no time for worry; I'm too busy." The yoke of Torah, as per the expression of the *berachah*, *"la'asok"*—to be busy with words of Torah—offers a certain emotional freedom to anyone willing to accept it.

ח. רבי אלעזר איש ברתותא אומר תן לו משלו שאתה ושלך שלו וכן בדוד הוא אומר כי ממך הכל ומידך נתנו לך.

Mishnah 8. Rabbi Elazar of Bartosa says: Give Him from that which is His, for you and what you have are His. And so did David [HaMelech] say, "For all is from You, and it is [what came to us] from Your Hand we have given You." [Divrei Hayamim I 29:14]

We live in an age of generational decline and verbal inflation. Whereas the term *"mesirus nefesh"* used to mean literally sacrificing life itself for Hashem (e.g., choosing death rather than worship idols), today the term is commonly used to praise anyone who gives up much time and comfort for Torah and mitzvos. Praiseworthy as such sacrifices are, Rabbi Elazar is saying that it can be made easier if we develop the attitude that "sacrifice" is not actually sacrificing anything at all.

Imagine someone who truly thinks of their own bank account as belonging totally to Hashem. The Divine Owner graciously allows him to take whatever he needs, but asks him to generously distribute a portion to other needy people as well. With that attitude, giving tzedakah is not a "sacrifice" but a naturally pleasant activity.

Such attitudes are not easy to develop, but many people adopt the stratagem of putting a percentage of every paycheck in a separate tzedakah account. Once deposited, it is no longer seen as "mine" and is much easier to give away wholeheartedly.

But Rabbi Elazar is not speaking only of money; "you *and* what you have are His." Rav Moshe Feinstein suggested that just as we find a halachah of *maaser*, giving a tenth of one's money, so too should we allocate giving to others (besides our families) a tenth of our *time*. Whether in community volunteer work or tutoring someone who needs help, if we budget 10% of our waking hours to do *chessed* and then ask ourselves how we might use the allocated time, we will seek out and find new opportunities to give of ourselves—and do so with a smile.

ט. רבי יעקב אומר המהלך בדרך ושונה ומפסיק ממשנתו ואומר מה נאה אילן זה מה נאה ניר זה מעלה עליו הכתוב כאלו מתחיב בנפשו.

Mishnah 9. Rabbi Yaakov says: One who walks on the road and reviews [his Torah learning], and interrupts his learning and says, "How beautiful is this tree! How beautiful is this plowed field!" the pasuk considers it as if he has sinned against his soul [or: forfeited his life].

The sin is *bitul Torah*—especially grievous for interrupting when he is already engaged in learning—but why give the example of admiring trees and plowed fields? We could answer that it means to say that interrupting one's learning is a sin even if he is doing so to admire Hashem's Creation. However, the plowed field was made not by Hashem but by humans, so why use it as the example?

Perhaps Rabbi Yaakov is warning us: Someone who interrupts his learning for trivia knows he is wasting his time and will hopefully regret it and improve in the future. But someone who interrupts learning to admire beauty, who is engaged in an aesthetic activity, may mistakenly believe it is a spiritual experience, i.e., an elevation of soul comparable to *talmud Torah.*

People who truly appreciate great art, classical music, or beautiful sunsets can be deeply moved by the experience, and a person of what used to be called high culture was considered a superior human being. I believe there is much to be said in favor of high culture, but Rabbi Yaakov warns us not to confuse the aesthetic with *ruchnius*, and certainly not to allow it to compete for our affection with *Toras Hashem.*

יא. רבי חנינא בן דוסא אומר כל שיראת חטאו קודמת לחכמתו חכמתו מתקימת. וכל שחכמתו קודמת ליראת חטאו אין חכמתו מתקימת.

Mishnah 11. Rabbi Chanina ben Dosa says: Anyone whose fear of sin precedes his wisdom, his wisdom will endure. But anyone whose wisdom precedes his fear of sin, his wisdom will not endure.

The word "precedes" may mean precedes in importance, i.e., takes priority in his scale of values. If he possesses fear of sin, he will feel the weight of responsibility upon him to correctly understand what he learns and to review regularly in order not to forget. If he lacks fear of sin, he may well be satisfied with superficial understanding and is less likely to make the effort to review.

The only problem (though I don't believe it is a major problem) is that the Mishnah does not refer to someone who lacks fear of sin. He does possess fear of sin, except that his love of wisdom is even greater than his *yiras cheit*. I wish *I* could be such a person! Why should his wisdom not endure?

But perhaps we should take the word "precedes" (*kodemes*) more literally, meaning precedes in *time*. And the word "wisdom" here is not simply a synonym for Torah learning but refers to the ability to analyze and probe deeply into the meaning of anything he examines (including Torah learning, of course).

That is, if a person does not yet possess very much wisdom or fear of sin, and he embarks on a program to work hard to develop first one and then the other, then he might well say: "It takes wisdom and great effort to even understand *yiras Hashem* (see Chapter 1 of *Mesillas Yesharim*), let alone to attain it. I will therefore focus first on attaining wisdom (*chochmah*) and afterwards work on *yirah* (*mussar*)."

Unfortunately, wisdom without fear of sin is a broken tool. Such a person will study *mussar sefarim* but focus only on those parts that interest him (as Rav Yaakov Kamenetsky said), or absorb *mussar* lessons but apply them only to other people. As a fellow who heard a talk from Rav Avigdor Miller told me, "He really gave it to them." "*Them.*"

But if fear of sin comes first, one immediately applies every lesson learned to oneself besides feeling the responsibility to understand the material correctly and thoroughly. Such is the wisdom that endures.

יב. הוא היה אומר כל שמעשיו מרובין מחכמתו חכמתו
מתקיימת. וכל שחכמתו מרבה ממעשיו אין חכמתו מתקיימת.

Mishnah 12. He used to say: Anyone whose [good] deeds exceed his wisdom, his wisdom will endure. But anyone whose wisdom exceeds his good deeds, his wisdom will not endure.

Some understand the Mishnah to be teaching that a wise person who is deficient in good deeds is seriously flawed, which is certainly true. But the Mishnah says, "anyone," meaning even someone who excels in both virtue *and* wisdom; nevertheless, if the level of his *chochmah* is higher than his *tzidkus*, he is in trouble. Why is this so?

> *For it is to the honor of the Torah that one who learns more of it progresses more, likewise, in righteousness and in refinement of character traits. Any lack in this respect in someone who learns a great deal contributes to a disparagement of learning itself, which is, G-d forbid, a desecration of His name (may He be blessed), Who gave us His holy Torah and commanded us to occupy ourselves with it in order to attain our perfection. (Mesillas Yesharim, chap. 11)*

To whatever degree one's Torah learning does not lead to action, it is more an academic study than *Toras Hashem*, and he risks forfeiting the *siyata d'Shmaya* necessary to succeed in the long run. Even without the supernatural aspect, if a scholar does not feel that every insight (in Torah learning or wisdom in general) must lead to action, then his academic study is ultimately not of supreme importance even to himself, and he will not delve deeply enough or review enough.

The other side of the coin is the person who seeks to do more and more good deeds. For him, every line he learns is an opportunity to discover what more he can do, how to do it in the best manner, and how to add depth of understanding to the deed. Such is the learning that endures.

יג. הוא היה אומר כל שרוח הבריות נוחה הימנו רוח המקום נוחה הימנו וכל שאין רוח הבריות נוחה הימנו אין רוח המקום נוחה הימנו.

Mishnah 13. He used to say: Anyone whom the spirit of other people is pleased with, the spirit of Hashem [HaMakom] is pleased with. And anyone whom the spirit of other people is not pleased with, the spirit of Hashem is not pleased with.

This is generally understood as coming to emphasize that meticulous observance in *mitzvos bein adam laMakom* without similar care for *mitzvos bein adam l'chaveiro* is not enough — something we all know (even if we do not always act accordingly). But the Mishnah is also saying much, much more.

The Mishnah is clearly implying that, "Anyone whom the spirit of other people is pleased with" — *even if he is somewhat deficient in mitzvah observance, nevertheless* — "the spirit of Hashem is pleased with him."

Hashem certainly judges every violation of every halachah, but Chazal have told us that the process of judgment can be more strict or less depending on how we treat others: "*Ha'maavir al midosav maavirin lo al kol p'shaav*," and one who is *dan l'kaf zechus* is judged by Hashem *l'kaf zechus* (this Mishnah may well be the source for those statements of Chazal). So treating others in the best possible way, besides its own intrinsic mitzvah value, also has a positive effect on the verdict on all our *mitzvos bein adam laMakom*.

But there is still more.

The Alter from Slabodka was once sitting with a few *talmidim*, and the name of Rav Isaac Sher (who eventually became the Alter's son-in-law and successor) came up. One *talmid* said: "Reb Isaac? A *geshmaker mensch*." Another *talmid* protested: "That's all? Reb Isaac is the *ari she'ba'chaburah* (the "lion" of the student body). The Alter smiled and said: "Is it a small thing to be a *geshmaker mensch*? The Mishnah says, 'Anyone who the spirit of other people is pleased with, the spirit of Hashem is pleased with.'"

A person can be a *tzaddik* and a *baal chessed* yet still not be *geshmak*—"succulent," luscious, enjoyable to be around (I suspect my *chassidishe* friends would smilingly place most Litvaks in that not-*geshmak* category). A yeshiva *rebbi* who is not only kind but also *warm* has a profound impact and will be fondly remembered by his *talmidim* all their lives.

So here is a new idea. Before next Yom Kippur, when we are thinking about resolutions for the coming year, why not consider resolving to become a *geshmaker mensch*, someone whose company others enjoy and whose smile lights up the room? That alone won't make you a *tzaddik*, but to be someone the spirit of Hashem is pleased with—is that a small thing?

יד. רבי דוסא בן הרכינס אומר שנה של שחרית ויין של צהרים ושיחת הילדים וישיבת בתי כנסיות של עמי הארץ מוציאין את האדם מן העולם.

Mishnah 14. Rabbi Dosa ben Horkinus says: Morning sleep, wine at midday, the conversation of children, and sitting in gatherings of the ignorant [amei ha'aretz] take a person out from the world.

"The world" might refer to *Olam Haba*, but if so, it should have said that these things prevent a person from *entering* the world (see Chapter 2, Mishnah 16). Therefore, the Mishnah must mean *this* world.

Picture a happily married man with a beautiful family, a successful career, and a respected position in his community who becomes a heroin addict and loses it all. Now destitute, homeless, friendless, and despairing, he has been taken out from his world—a world of joy and achievement—and relocated to a world that is hardly a world at all.

The Mishnah is coming to caution us that some relatively small things—patterns of behavior that are detrimental without being halachically forbidden—can in time have devastating effects.

- "Morning sleep"—When the day gets off to a strong start, e.g., learning before *Shacharis* followed by unrushed davening, it sets the tone for the rest of the day. Arising late sometimes means playing catch-up the rest of the day, and as a daily routine it can lead to ruin.

- "Wine at midday"—Most people (according to some studies, especially teachers and students) are more productive in the morning than in the afternoon; but after a three-martini lunch, virtually everyone's productivity goes downhill the rest of the day.

- "The conversation of children"—This does not mean speaking with children (a vital part of parenting), but childish talk that is the standard conversation for so many adults. Topics like sports, entertainment (even Orthodox entertainment), politics, gossip, all interlaced with cliches and pointless one-line jokes without wit—for too many people, "small talk" unbecoming of a wise or dignified person is the only sort of talk they know. Regardless of topic, attempts to offer thoughtful insight are rare, and, like small children, people will say the first thing that pops into their heads, sometimes merely to hear the sound of their own voices. Empty talk, even if not forbidden, tends to empty the head as well.

- "Sitting in gatherings of the *amei ha'aretz*"—As the *Rambam* writes in *Hilchos De'os*, it is the nature of human beings to be drawn after the opinions, attitudes, and actions of people with whom he associates. *Amei ha'aretz*, even if mitzvah observant, do not spend time in serious Torah study, which invariably leads them to not value serious Torah study, and they are unable to look at the world through Torah lenses. Spending time with them more than necessary must affect our own values and attitudes, and we become different people without realizing it.

טו. רבי אלעזר המודעי אומר המחלל את הקדשים והמבזה את המועדות והמלבין פני חברו ברבים והמפר בריתו של אברהם אבינו והמגלה פנים בתורה שלא כהלכה אף על פי שיש בידו תורה ומעשים טובים אין לו חלק לעולם הבא.

Mishnah 15. Rabbi Elazar HaModai says: One who desecrates holy things, and [more likely: or] disgraces the festivals, who embarrasses his friend in public, who nullifies the covenant of Avraham Avinu, or who perverts the Torah contrary to halachah, even if he possesses Torah and good deeds, he has no share in the World to Come.

Picture Beryl and Shmeryl, two Jewish men who unfortunately ignore or transgress a number of important halachos. When asked about it, Beryl offers no excuse except laziness or lust, while Shmeryl defends his behavior by shrugging off or making light of the mitzvos he does not observe. Even if their *actions* are identical, their *attitudes* make a world (literally!) of difference.

The Mishnah is saying that *respect* is an essential component of Yiddishkeit, and a lack of respect denies one entrance to the World to Come. This applies even to a halachah like Chol Hamoed ("disgraces the festivals"), which is only *mi'd'Rabanan.*

Interestingly, it applies also to embarrassing a fellow Jew. Perhaps the reason for this is that embarrassing a teammate shows a lack of respect for the team, and a lack of respect for the goals of Torah and *kavod Shamayim* to which the team is dedicated.

Now consider a new idea: If respect is so vital that a lack of it can deny entrance to *Olam Haba* to a man who has Torah and good deeds, then isn't it probable that having respect can gain entrance to *Olam*

Haba for a man who does *not* have Torah and good deeds (or at least not very many of them)? To develop an attitude and a habit of speaking and acting with great respect for the Torah and for *b'nei Torah* might be a source of enormous *zechus* at the cost of relatively little effort.

If I recall correctly, Rav Avigdor Miller had a lecture entitled, "Ten Steps to Greatness." One of those steps was—when no one is around to see you—sit on the floor for a moment as a sign of mourning for the Beis Hamikdash. You don't feel mourning? It's not even Tishah B'Av? No matter. It's a gesture of respect, and Rav Miller considered it a step to greatness.

טז. רבי ישמעאל אומר הוי קל לראש ונוח לתשחורת והוי מקבל
את כל האדם בשמחה.

Mishnah 16. Rabbi Yishmael says: Be yielding to a superior, easy-going with the young, and receive every person with simchah.

The Mishnah is telling us how to deal with different sorts of people—in ways that are *chessed* for them and that foster a sense of contentment within ourselves.

"Be yielding to a superior"—You may not like your boss, but if you're stuck with him, "yield" emotionally, giving in and going along without resentment.

"Easy-going with the young"—Exasperating as young people sometimes are, keep in mind that they are ignorant about so very many things, so put up with their foolishness, and don't let it bother you. After all, if he's only ten (or twenty, or thirty, or forty) years old, how much should you expect him to understand?

"And receive every person with *simchah*"—Someone comes to see you—perhaps it is not the most convenient time; perhaps he wants a favor. Nevertheless, act as if you're happy to see him. We all want to be liked, and we all want others to think well of us, and if we go to visit someone (especially if it's to ask a favor), it means a great deal to be welcomed cheerfully.

A question: In Chapter 1, Shammai said, "Receive every person with a cheerful countenance." In our Mishnah, "receiving with *simchah*" seems to be something more. Rabbi Yishmael might be disagreeing with Shammai, but if he does not disagree (it is generally assumed that Mishnayos in *Avos* do agree with one another), why the different phrase?

Perhaps the two Mishnayos complement each other: Shammai is speaking of an action, while Rabbi Yishmael is referring to an attitude. Shammai: Whether or not you are happy to see someone, it's a kindness to greet them with a smile. Rabbi Yishmael: When someone comes to speak with you, be happy that they've come; if they are not coming to ask a favor but want only your conversation or your company, be happy that you are liked, and if they come to ask a favor, be happy that you are *needed*. Everyone I meet enriches me in some way, and realizing it gives me a joy I am happy to share.

יז. רבי עקיבא אומר שחוק וקלות ראש מרגילין את האדם לערוה.
מסורת סיג לתורה מעשרות סיג לעושר נדרים סיג לפרישות סיג
לחכמה שתיקה.

Mishnah 17. Rabbi Akiva says: Joking or mockery [s'chok] and light-headedness or levity [kalus rosh] accustom a man to sexual sins. Masores is a [protective] fence for the Torah; tithes are a fence for wealth; vows are a fence for abstinence; a fence for wisdom is silence.

The theme of this Mishnah is the need for protective fences, and Rabbi Akiva forcefully makes his point by first giving an example how the absence of such fences can lead to catastrophe. The right joke at the right time is a "small excellency" (Samuel Johnson), and more than one insightful witticism of Rav Aharon Kotler has been passed down by generations of Lakewood *talmidim*. But some people fall into the habit of treating *everything* as a joke (with or without mockery). You cannot speak with them about any serious matter (as *Mesillas Yesharim* writes, they are like a drowning man), and eventually all moral barriers are broken down.

(A point often overlooked is that *s'chok v'kalus rosh* are themselves key elements in the moral collapse of Western civilization, and it can be useful to read letters and biographies of nineteenth-century political leaders to contrast their sense of dignity and seriousness with the leaders of today.)

"*Masores*"—is our carefully handed-down tradition telling us the exact words of the Torah, down to which words include or omit letters like *vav* and *yud*. Different manuscripts of Talmud and the siddur differ in many details, sometimes leading to major controversies. But all Jews have the same *Chumash* with the same mitzvos, thanks to the *masores* that has served as a protective fence through the ages.

"Tithes are a fence for wealth"—In *Hilchos Teshuvah*, the *Rambam* writes that the blessings Hashem promises (in the second paragraph of the *Shema*, for instance) are not rewards that are given only in the World to Come. Rather, if we use our material wealth for good (e.g., tzedakah), Hashem will give us more wealth to enable us to do more to serve Him. If we do not use our wealth for good, or if wealth causes us to forget Hashem, Hashem may take it all away. Therefore, to protect the wealth we were blessed with (and compared to former generations, all of us today are wealthy), giving significant amounts for mitzvah purposes (tithes) is insurance that our wealth should remain intact and possibly increase over time.

"Vows are a fence for abstinence"—Let's say you wish to refrain from speaking *lashon hara*, but your willpower is weak. If you make a vow (and fully appreciate the severity of breaking a vow), that may give you the boost you need to succeed.

I know someone who had trouble losing weight who finally succeeded by accepting upon himself vows of voluntary fast days. But even if you believe this would work for you (perhaps in modified form, like a vow to abstain from eating certain unhealthy foods, and making vows to last for only a week at a time), its practical application is very limited and for most people strictly forbidden. A smoker who vows to quit may very well fail and thereby commit the serious transgression of breaking a vow. And a vow to refrain from speaking *lashon hara* requires such constant and intense vigilance that the vow will inevitably be broken numerous times.

The *sefer Divrei Yehoshua* (Rav Yehoshua Heller, a *talmid* of Rav Yisrael Salanter) suggests the following: Rather than vowing to keep to your resolution, vow that each time you break it, you will give a certain amount of money to tzedakah (enough to hurt, but not enough to bankrupt you). A modified version of this is not to make an actual vow but merely a commitment to give the money each time you break your resolution. This sensitizes us and heightens our awareness of our actions, reinforcing our resolve.

"A fence for wisdom is silence"—The man or woman habituated to silence thinks before speaking (ask yourself: How often do I pause before speaking to consider what I should or should not say?) and is less likely to utter something foolish. The naturally silent person does not interrupt another person who is speaking and is able to absorb what he hears and benefit from it (based on Rabbeinu Yonah). But these behaviors are more by way of aids to acquiring wisdom than they are fences to protect the wisdom we already have.

Another explanation, which well explains the nature of this protective fence, is the *Maharal* in *Nesivos Olam* that I discussed above in Chapter 1, Mishnah 17. It is worth reading again.

יח. הוא היה אומר חביב אדם שנברא בצלם. חיבה יתרה נודעת
לו שנברא בצלם שנאמר כי בצלם אלקים עשה את האדם.

Mishnah 18. He used to say: Beloved is man, for he was created in [Hashem's] image; it is an extra measure of love that it was made known to him that he was created in [Hashem's] image, as it is said, "For in the image of G-d He made man."

We do not know that multiple Mishnayos said by one Tanna are necessarily related (although we should assume that multiple statements in the same Mishnah are related, and we do try to determine what the relationship might be). But it is not too great a stretch to suggest that after Mishnah 17, which emphasizes human weakness and the ever-present need for protective fences, in Mishnah 18 Rabbi Akiva encourages us by teaching us the greatness of every individual.

"Beloved is man, for he was created in Hashem's image"—Since Hashem has no physical form, "image" might refer to the uniquely human capacities for rational thought, free will, and a moral sense. However, in order to achieve the goal of Creation (see the opening chapters of *Derech Hashem*), it was necessary to create human beings with those attributes, and since they are necessary, our being endowed with them does not seem to indicate special love. *Tzelem Elokim* (Hashem's image) must therefore mean something more. What is that something?

In explaining this term, *Rashi* (*Bereishis* 1:27) writes: "*Tzelem d'mus Yotzro*—Image of the semblance of the Creator." But what does that mean? I heard from my *rebbeim* (and I pray that I understood correctly) the following:

An artist can draw a picture of a person who is happy, sad, or angry, but to draw a picture of happiness, sadness, or anger—the emotions themselves, not attached to a person—would seem to be impossible. And yet if we look at two abstract paintings—one filled with zig-zag strokes of red and yellow, and the other with green circles—and we are told that one painting represents anger and the other contentment, most people would agree which was which.

In a similar way, if the greatest artist in history, i.e., Hashem the Creator, would draw a picture or craft a sculpture representing Hashem (who has no physical form) as accurately as possible, that artistic creation would be—the human face. This was not necessary for us to be able to serve Hashem and complete our mission on earth, but Hashem made us this way as an act of love for every human being.

"It is even greater love that it was made known to him that he was created in Hashem's image"—I have photographs of my grandchildren on the door of our refrigerator because I love them, and when they come to visit, I make a point of showing them that I have their photographs so that they should know how much I love them.

The Mishnah is teaching: The Torah says we are created in Hashem's image because Hashem not only loves us, but wants us to *know* that He loves us. And when in the Torah He calls us His children, it is not only because He loves us like a parent loves a child but also because He wants us to know it.

חביבין ישראל שנתן להם כלי חמדה...שנאמר כי לקח טוב נתתי
לכם תורתי אל תעזובו.

Beloved are Israel, for a cherished instrument [the Torah] was given to them...as it is said, "For I have given you a good teaching, do not forsake My Torah."

The Torah, the greatest gift ever given, can surely be seen as a sign of love, but why is it called "a cherished instrument" (*kli chemdah*), and why is this "instrument" aspect the sign of special love?

The Torah tells us the mitzvos that we are commanded to keep in order to do Hashem's will and to earn eternal reward in *Olam Haba*. This would be an infinitely precious gift, even if we could not learn from the Torah anything that would make us wiser, happier, or more ethically sensitive. But the fact is that the Torah (properly studied and properly practiced) is a "cherished instrument" that *does* make us wiser, happier, and more ethically sensitive, and that Hashem gave us a Torah that accomplishes all these "extras," is a sign of special love.

"For I have given you a good teaching, do not forsake My Torah"—How do we see from here that the Torah is a precious instrument? Perhaps it is from the word "good." It is (or at least should be) self-evident that the book that teaches us how to do Hashem's will and merit eternal reward is good, and so there is no need for the *pasuk* to say it. But it means: Not only is the Torah good because it guides us to achieve the goal of existence, but it is also *good in itself*—elevating us in all sorts of ways as we study and practice it every day.

Some manuscripts read: "A cherished instrument through which the world was created," that the Torah is the blueprint for the universe, as it says, "He looked in the Torah and created the universe" (*Midrash Rabbah*). According to this version, the special love is that in learning and keeping the Torah, we are not only doing Hashem's will but are also living in a way that puts us in harmony with the universe. And since the *sefarim* say that a human being is the universe in microcosm (*olam katan*), learning and keeping the Torah properly will give us the serenity of being in complete harmony with ourselves.

יט. הכל צפוי והרשות נתונה נתונה ובטוב העולם נדון והכל לפי רוב
המעשה.

Mishnah 19. Everything is foreseen, yet free will is granted. The world is judged with goodness. And everything is according to the abundance of deeds.

"Everything is foreseen, yet free will is granted"—A famous philosophical question posed by the *Rambam* and others is: If Hashem knows the future, then He knows what choices we will make every moment of our lives. But if He knows in advance what choices we will make, then (it can be argued that) those choices are pre-determined, which means we do not have free will to choose otherwise.

More than one answer has been given to this question (and I confess that, not being philosophically minded myself, the question does not bother me at all). But the Mishnah is coming to tell us, whether you know the answer or not, it is not a problem. We do indeed have free will (so don't say what one young man said to me, "I'm not religious—it must be *bashert*"), and yet Hashem does indeed know the future.

It may appear that this is asking us to live with two contradictory ideas (though possibly the contradiction is only apparent but not real). But Rav Avigdor Miller taught that this is a principle of the Torah (and I would add, one of the secrets of the Torah)—that we must sometimes live with ideas that contain great truths, even if they appear contradictory.

Rav Miller's example was: We know Hashem is pleased when we do His Will ("*yismach Hashem b'maasav*") and saddened when we must be punished ("*kalani mi'zro'i*," see Mishnah *Sanhedrin* 6:5), yet we also know that, being Perfect, Hashem is not subject to human emotions, i.e., not dependent on our actions for His happiness. To believe that we can make Hashem happy or sad may be pure heresy. Yet, we are to act as if (and to feel that) Hashem is happy or sad when His children do what is right or not.

(Another example: the *Chayei Adam* writes that we are to think of our parents as great and honored people—*tzaddikim v'nichbadei aretz*—whether they are or not.)

"THE WORLD IS JUDGED with goodness"—Ultimately, Hashem judges all of us according to what we deserve, and there is no escaping it (*Ramchal* in *Mesillas Yesharim*), yet Hashem also seeks ways to help us receive a favorable verdict without perverting justice (also *Ramchal,* in *Derech Hashem*), such as a child's good deeds giving merit to the parent, or the soul being sent back to earth to live again (*gilgul ha'neshamah*) to make up for sins committed the first time.

This phrase seems unconnected to the beginning of the Mishnah: "Everything is foreseen yet free will is given." But perhaps the connection is: Even if we have complete free will, since Hashem knew in advance who is going to end up a spiritual failure, isn't it arguable that it was *chas v'shalom* unfair to have this person be born and eventually punished for his sins? To this unspoken question, the Mishnah answers:

1. The world is judged with goodness, and in the big picture, even the failure will learn that his few mitzvos made life more than worthwhile.

2. Everything is according to the abundance of deeds, meaning even a sinner whose good deeds outnumber his bad ones is judged as a *tzaddik* (*Rambam*, based on the Gemara).

Now, granted that major sins count more than minor mitzvos—but Torah study (for example) is a major mitzvah, and *every word* of Torah is an additional mitzvah (Vilna Gaon). In the course of a year, the words of *pesukim* in daily davening alone add up to hundreds of thousands of mitzvos, so on balance, give thanks that you were born.

The *Rambam* explains "everything is according to the abundance of deeds" differently. Just as a daily half-hour of exercise is better than four hours of exercise once a week, so too is giving a dollar a day to tzedakah better than giving seven dollars once a week. Apart from the relative merits of seven small mitzvos versus one larger mitzvah, the daily *habit* of doing good is what refines our character over the long term.

כ. הוא היה אומר הכל נתון בערבון ומצודה פרוסה על כל
החיים...והדין דין אמת והכל מתוקן לסעודה.

Mishnah 20. He used to say: Everything is given on collateral, and a net is spread over all the living...the judgment is a judgment of truth, and everything is prepared for the banquet.

"Everything is given on collateral"—This means that we must pay for all the infinite number of blessings Hashem gives us every moment. We "pay" by using our blessings to help us better serve Hashem, or we pay in the World to Come by giving up the reward we would otherwise receive for the mitzvos we did while alive, leaving us little or nothing for which to be rewarded in eternity.

It is a stern judgment, and we cannot escape it—"a net is spread over all the living"—and yet "the judgment is a judgment of truth," which raises the question: If we have no choice in the matter, why is the judgment so stern, especially since Rabbi Akiva himself in the previous Mishnah said that "the world is judged with goodness"?

Perhaps the explanation is that there is more than one type of payment that is acceptable (though some types are superior to others).

Hashem does not need any of our mitzvos, so in what way is doing a mitzvah "payment" to Him? The answer is that all our mitzvos are expressions of gratitude, and it is the showing of gratitude that is the method of payment, like the loving parent who gives his children gifts and seeks nothing in return but very much wants the children to say "Thank you" for their own good.

But if all service of Hashem is a form of gratitude, then even if we don't use every blessing the way it is meant to be used—e.g., if we don't use our material possessions to give as much tzedakah as we should—but we do make a point of saying a heartfelt "Thank you, Hashem!" every chance we get, then we have also "paid" for our blessings by using them (to some extent) for the purpose for which they were given.

The "net is spread" and we must pay, but giving thanks to Hashem for the multitude of blessings is a payment everyone can afford to make without hardship. Chazal got us started on this by mandating a minimum of a hundred *berachos* to recite each day.

(This gives us a deeper understanding of the *pasuk*, "And now, Israel, what (*mah*) does Hashem ask of you, only…" etc., on which Chazal commented that the word "*mah*" hints at "*me'ah*," (a hundred) *berachos*. The word "only" indicates that what Hashem asks is not difficult, but the *pasuk* goes on to list five wide-ranging areas of service. The implication is that although a great deal is asked of us, there is also a relatively easy way we can comply, at least to some extent. Since all service to Hashem is an expression of gratitude, Chazal interpreted the "easy way" to also mean expressing gratitude and instituted *berachos* to show us the way to the "prepared feast" in eternity.)

כא. רבי אלעזר בן עזריה אומר אם אין תורה אין דרך ארץ אם אין דרך ארץ אין תורה אם אין חכמה אין יראה אם אין יראה אין חכמה אם אין דעת אין בינה אם אין בינה אין דעת אם אין קמח אין תורה אם אין תורה אין קמח.

Mishnah 21. Rabbi Elazar ben Azariah says: If there is no Torah, there is no derech eretz; if there is no derech eretz, there is no Torah. If there is no wisdom, there is no fear [of Hashem]; if there is no fear, there is no wisdom. If there is no daas, there is no binah; if there is no binah, there is no daas. If there is no flour, there is no Torah; if there is no Torah, there is no flour.

In Chapter 2, Mishnah 2, *derech eretz* meant worldly occupation, making a living. But here the term *derech eretz* refers to all the obligations of a human being (not necessarily Jewish) who knows there is a G-d in the world, that G-d created us in His image, and that we must act as befits our special status, avoiding "conduct unbecoming" a *tzelem Elokim*.

"If there is no *derech eretz*, there is no Torah" because, as Rav Avigdor Miller put it, the Torah is the second story of a two-story building, with *derech eretz* being the first story (I believe Rav Samson Raphael Hirsch expressed a similar idea when he wrote that a Jew is Man-Israelite, *Mensch-Yisrael*.) A Jew who lacks *derech eretz* may learn a lot and do many mitzvos, but what he is engaged in cannot truly be called *Toras Hashem*. (I think it worth noting that if we take this seriously, it changes the way we look at a great many things.)

But "if there is no Torah, there is no *derech eretz*" either because we will end up adjusting our standards of behavior to fit our desires and prejudices. The old-time English gentleman was educated in the highest standards of propriety, but that did not preclude blatant racial and religious prejudice, discreet adultery, and the rule that "a gentleman is never rude by accident."

"IF THERE IS NO WISDOM, there is no fear [of Hashem]"—"If you seek it like silver, and search for it like buried treasure, (only) then will you understand fear of Hashem" (*Mishlei* 2:4–5) and "Indeed, fear of Hashem is wisdom" (*Iyov* 28:28). The Introduction to *Mesillas Yesharim* elaborates on this—that it takes wisdom just to know what fear of Hashem is, let alone to achieve it.

(Granted that achieving *yiras Hashem* requires great effort and great wisdom, but is it truly so hard to understand what *yirah* is? If we read the chapter in *Mesillas Yesharim* where he explains it, isn't that enough to understand the subject? But the Alter from Slabodka wrote that even very learned Jews who had never studied under Rav Simcha Zissel of Kelm did not know what Judaism is all about (*tzuras haTorah*), and their perception of Judaism is the *opposite* of what it actually is. Difficult as it may be to fully accept what he wrote, it nevertheless indicates that there is a depth to these matters of which we are completely unaware.)

"If there is no fear (of Hashem), there is no wisdom" for two reasons: One is that the pursuit of wisdom requires enormous effort, freedom from bias (the desire to have the facts lead to a particular conclusion), the humility to admit error, and the sense of responsibility engendered by fear of Hashem is a necessary prerequisite for all of these. And second, someone without fear of Hashem does not truly understand the meaning of life, the meaning of history, the wisdom and kindliness of all Creation, or human frailty and perverseness, and therefore lacks the foundations to achieve any sort of true wisdom.

"IF THERE IS NO *DAAS*, there is no *binah*; if there is no *binah*, there is no *daas*"—*Binah* means the ability to analyze, "*l'havin davar mi'toch davar.*" *Daas* is knowledge we have internalized so that it has become an integral part of our thinking.

For instance, a typical high-school yeshiva student has learned enough mathematics to know that one-fifth of 40 is 8, and adding a fifth to 40 equals 48. Then he learns that in Chazal's reckoning, "adding a fifth" means dividing the number into four equal parts and adding one more equal part for a total of five, so "adding a fifth" to 40 equals 50. Even after he understands it, it will take a long time to become fully comfortable and internalize it. If he encounters a Gemara about "adding a third to ten," he will slowly calculate: "10 plus one-third is 13, and 1/3…no, the Gemara means adding an amount to 10 that will be 1/3 of the total, so it means adding 5."

He understands the Gemara's system of reckoning, but it is not fully a part of him, and until it becomes part of him, it will be very difficult to analyze a *sugya* in which such addition is an important factor. His knowledge of it is not yet *daas*, and "if there is no *daas*, there is no *binah*."

But the way to attain *daas* of a subject is to turn it over and over in our minds, seeking its underlying reasoning, and exploring its various permutation ("In this system, how much is one-sixth added to five, or subtracted from seven, or one-third added to a half, etc.). Thus we apply *binah* to the little bit we know to come to *daas*, and once we have *daas* in the various parts of the *sugya*, we can then try to analyze—*binah*—the whole.

"IF THERE IS NO FLOUR, there is no Torah"—I heard that a certain famous *tzaddik* in Eretz Yisrael, who believed that American *b'nei Torah* who could move to Eretz Yisrael should do so, nevertheless did not encourage his American son-in-law (a noted *talmid chacham*) to make the move. He explained: My son-in-law will be hard-pressed to make a living in Eretz Yisrael, and that will harm his *ruchniyus* (spiritual state).

Note that he was not worried about his son-in-law's inability to make a living *per se*, but that lack of *parnassah* would create a strain with harmful spiritual effect. The Gemara says that a man with enough food for today who feels anxiety about tomorrow is lacking in faith, but the fact is that anxiety affects learning and observance, and one must see to it that he has the necessities of life, the definition of "necessities" varying from person to person.

"IF THERE IS NO TORAH, there is no flour"—This seems to say that a person who does not learn Torah will not be able to earn a living, but that is contradicted by our experience. (However, one could take it to mean that without the merit of Torah, one does not *deserve* to make a living, and any success he has comes only at the cost of his losing *Olam Haba*.) It is also odd that the Mishnah says "flour" rather than bread or food.

Perhaps the meaning is: Hashem is *"Ha'zan es ha'kol*—He provides food for all," but the Gemara says, *"Am ha'aretz assur le'echol basar*—Someone who does not study Torah is forbidden to eat meat, because what right does he have to take an animal's life if he does not live more than an animal life himself?

In a similar way, animals eat foods only in their raw state, and it is an extra gift from Hashem that we can process grain into flour to bake bread or cake (this is why there is a mitzvah to take *challah* even if tithes had already been separated from the grain). If a person does not study Torah and lives only an animal life, how does he deserve this extra gift? (The Mishnah could have said "bread" rather than flour, but we would then have thought he is making the point of bread as a staple food and not the benefit of being processed.)

Chapter Four

א. בן זומא אומר איזהו חכם הלומד מכל אדם...איזהו גבור הכובש את יצרו...איזהו עשיר השמח בחלקו...איזהו מכובד המכבד את הבריות...

Mishnah 1. Ben Zoma says: Who is wise? He who learns from every person...Who is mighty? He who conquers his passions [yitzro]...Who is rich? He who is happy with his portion...Who is honored? He who honors human beings [beriyos]...

The four different points in this Mishnah are brought out with four similar questions, implying that they revolve around a single theme. Before attempting to identify the theme, do we understand the Mishnah on even a simple level?

"Who is wise? He who learns from every person"—Visit any yeshiva and ask: Picture a brilliant and diligent *lamdan* who studies Torah day and night, who knows the entire Talmud and who has published *sefarim* on both Gemara and practical halachah, who respects his *rebbeim* and learns with *chavrusos*, but who does not learn from every person. Now picture a young yeshiva student of only average intelligence and diligence, who knows little and has published not at all, but he does try to learn from every person. Which of the two is more likely to be considered a *chacham* (wise man)?

So, is the Mishnah meant to be taken seriously? If it is, why does no one do it? Or might the Mishnah mean something else, perhaps something more subtle and profound?

"Who is honored? He who honors human beings"—I would understand the Mishnah had it said, "Who is *honorable*," meaning deserving
of honor, but *honored*? Society honors people of great achievement:
Torah scholars, rich people, politicians, or athletes (depending on the
social circles you move in). A poor "nobody" who honors other people
may be well-liked as a "nice guy," but is unlikely to receive an award at
your shul's annual dinner.

But the true meaning of this Mishnah can be found in the commentary of the *Maharal*, as explained in a letter of Rav Yerucham Levovitz.
Let's examine this one step at a time.

Virtually all young men and most young women want to grow up
to achieve something or become someone important, and too many
older people live lives of sadness surrounded by the wreckage of broken
dreams. Throughout history, the following four types have been viewed
as models of success to emulate:

1. The philosopher or wise man—Philosophy is not much admired
   today, and Torah Jews often associate it with heresy, but for
   millennia, philosophers were looked up to as almost a higher
   class of human beings—rare individuals who rise above petty
   material pursuits in their search for, and love of, wisdom (the
   word "philosopher" literally means "lover of wisdom").

2. The military hero—For much of history, war or the threat of war
   was part of daily life, and battle meant hand-to-hand combat.
   One heroic knight could overcome hordes of peasants and win
   renown as a savior of his people. Legendary names like Achilles
   and Sir Lancelot live on in world literature to this day.

3. The man or woman of wealth.

4. The man or woman who is honored by others—Throughout history, honors were given to people of outstanding achievement or
   to people of noble birth. Aristocrats were seen as higher sorts of
   people with "blue blood," elevated above the commoners. Even
   writers, artists, and athletes were viewed as somewhat higher,
   which explains why non-Jewish society forgives them for their
   immoral behavior that would not be tolerated in others.

Philosopher, hero, rich man, and nobleman—four paths to success and happiness, and for most people, all of them are hopelessly out of reach. How many people are blessed with the intelligence and the teachers to train them to become philosophers? How many have the strength and courage to become knightly heroes? We all try to make money, but few become rich, and outstanding achievement or being born to the nobility is almost always beyond our control.

Along comes our Mishnah to teach us that these four types of happiness are truly accessible—to everyone.

"Who is a wise man/philosopher?" The ancient philosopher was admired and seen as a higher sort of person because he truly loved wisdom, and the Mishnah is saying that this elevated status is available to all of us if we choose to become *"lovers of wisdom."* How do we do this? By subordinating other drives (like ego) to the search for wisdom, which we do by committing ourselves to "learn from every person," even if we might think it beneath our dignity to do so. Of course, you will not receive the praise and admiration the public gives to famous philosophers, but if your main goal is status, then you are not seeking to become that higher sort of person who loves wisdom, but something entirely different.

"Who is mighty?" (or better, "Who is a hero?") Heroes are admired not only for their muscles and skills, but they are admired above all for their courage and persistence in the face of adversity. To fight tirelessly against overwhelming odds and never surrender—that is what we most look up to. Invincible Superman would be far less attractive if he were not susceptible to being defeated by Kryptonite.

But if courage, persistence, and refusal to surrender are what we admire about heroes, then all of us can aspire to do deeds of valor on the field of battle against our personal *yetzer hara*. To "conquer our passions," to fight to overcome lust and anger and laziness throughout the day, and arise the next morning to do it all over again, that is Herculean heroism, and the achievement and grandeur young men dream of can truly be theirs.

"Who is rich?"—More than once, I have attended a *Pirkei Avos shiur* and heard the speaker say that "the Torah's definition of wealth is not money; it's being happy with what you have." Each time, I wanted to scream, "Maybe so, but I want wealth according to *my* definition of wealth, and that means money!" Surely, the Mishnah is not playing word games, and it uses the word "rich" the same way we do.

However, *why* do we want to be wealthy? Obviously, to be able to obtain all the things we desire, money being only the means to that end. If you were marooned on a desert island with heaps of cash but nothing available for purchase, you would not think of yourself as rich. On the other hand, if you possessed literally every single thing you desired, money would be unnecessary, and you would have no need to keep any around.

The *joy* of being rich (not spiritually rich, or Torah rich, but plain old rich rich) is that we have every single thing we want. That identical joy is available to *anyone* if he can only learn to "be happy with his portion," whatever he or she already has (even richer, really, because money cannot buy everything we desire). Note that this is not intended as a second-rate substitute for wealth but as the only way to obtain what the wealth-seeker really wants.

"Who is honored"—If you hired total strangers to stand up and applaud you, you would not feel honored (at least I hope not!). We love gestures of honor not for themselves, but because they signify that, for some reason, there is honor that we deserve. Honors proclaim that the recipient is in some way elevated on some higher level than the masses (even yeshiva dinner chairmen speak of "paying tribute" to honorees, and I heard one MC announce that we were assembled "to pay homage," though he did not ask us to actually bow our heads and kneel).

But since the joy of being honored is the feeling that you are elevated, it follows that a perceptive person who is indeed elevated would feel that same joy whether others recognized it or not. Is it possible for an ordinary person with no special talent or accomplishment to feel that elevation, and that it be based on something real? The Mishnah says that it is.

"Who is honored? He who honors human beings." Why should we honor human beings who are not outstanding in any way? Because all of them, all people, are *beriyos*, Hashem's *creations*.

Visitors to Paris who view Leonardo da Vinci's Mona Lisa tend to feel a respect for the painting; even if they know nothing about art, they are aware that it was created by one of the world's greatest artists, and that the painting is unique and priceless. So too, the connoisseur of Hashem's creations recognizes that each human being is unique, possessing a soul that is priceless, created with infinite wisdom by the Greatest of the Old Masters. He feels reverence for the Creator, and therefore respect for the human who is His Handiwork.

But someone who sees others this way will also see *himself* this way, for he too is a Divine masterpiece. Such a person lives in a different world from most of us—a much more elevated world—and he is no less elevated for perceiving that other people live there too.

The Mishnah is not offering a substitute for honor. It is offering the special feeling that we mortals derive *from* honor, i.e., to know that we have truly risen higher. And this achievement is accessible to everyone who chooses to "honor *beriyos*."

HAVING EXAMINED AND CONSIDERED the Mishnah's four points, we can now ask: What is its theme, the sum of its parts? It is that we can all find happiness and success within *ourselves*, and we need not—and should not—allow our happiness to depend on external factors or circumstances; and with this understanding, "thank Hashem, I am happy, always" (Rav Yerucham Levovitz).

ב. בן עזאי אומר הוי רץ למצוה קלה ובורח מן העבירה שמצוה
גוררת מצוה ועבירה גוררת עבירה ששכר מצוה מצוה ושכר
עבירה עבירה.

Mishnah 2. Ben Azzai says: Run to [perform even] a minor mitzvah, and flee from a transgression. For a mitzvah draws along another mitzvah, and a transgression draws along another transgression; for the reward of a mitzvah is a mitzvah, and the "reward" of a transgression is a transgression.

A simple (and not incorrect) way to understand this Mishnah is psychological—that doing mitzvos strengthens the self-image of "I'm *frum*," making it easier to do mitzvos in the future because that's the sort of person I am. The same is true of sins; if I commit even a small sin, then when I am next tempted, the little voice inside says, "Well, you're not so *frum* anyway."

But after pointing out that one mitzvah leads to another, what does Ben Azai add with the words "For the reward of a mitzvah is a mitzvah"? If he means that one mitzvah leads to another, he already said it; and if he means that the *only* reward for a mitzvah is that it encourages us to do another, is it true that there is no other reward for mitzvos?

Rather, the Mishnah is explaining that the reason one mitzvah leads to another (or one sin to another) is not only psychological but also spiritual. A farmer who works his fields and eats what he produces enjoys the direct result of his labor, and anyone whose health improves as a result of exercise benefits as a direct result of exercise. But in most jobs (doctor, lawyer, candlestick-maker), someone pays you for your work, but the pay does not come directly from the work itself unless you print money for a living.

Some people think that mitzvos are gold stars (and sins are black marks) in Hashem's "Notebook," and Hashem tallies up the gold stars and then rewards accordingly, i.e., the reward or punishment is not a direct result of our actions. Ben Azai tells us this is not so. "The reward of a mitzvah is a mitzvah" means that every mitzvah is nutrition for the soul, and in the Next World, the soul shines as a direct result of each mitzvah. A sin, though, is a pollutant that does injury to the soul even without special Divine punishment.

We do not see this shining or darkening of the soul in this life—if we did, we would all be saintly and free will would be lost—except in one way: Even the smallest mitzvah adds strength to the soul, making it easier to do more mitzvos, and sins have the opposite effect. So "a mitzvah brings along another mitzvah," *because* of the effect the mitzvah has on the soul; the reward of a mitzvah is the power of the mitzvah itself, in both this World and the Next.

ג. הוא היה אומר אל תהי בז לכל אדם ואל תהי מפליג לכל דבר שאין לך אדם שאין לו שעה ואין לך דבר שאין לו מקום.

Mishnah 3. He used to say: Do not despise any person, and do not be disdainful of any thing, for there is no person who does not have his hour, and there is no thing that does not have its place.

The Hebrew word "*mevazeh*" means "to treat someone scornfully," and we have already learned from Hillel (Chapter 1, Mishnah 12), Rabbi Yishmael (3:16) and Ben Zoma (4:1) not to act this way toward any person. But "*baz*" is to be scornful in the *mind*—to think that any person or thing as worthless. This too we should not do, because everything has its place in Hashem's plan, as do we.

It is an important principle that we live our lives on two levels: We are put here on earth to make moral choices (*Mesillas Yesharim*, Chapter 1), hopefully the right ones. But even when we fall short, life has a second level—in that Hashem *uses* our choices (even the wrong choices) in His plan for the world, thus giving us all a measure of redemption.

Ellen Willis was a rock 'n roll music critic for *Rolling Stone* magazine, with no connection with or interest in Orthodox Judaism. When Willis' brother became a *baal teshuvah* through Aish HaTorah, and her frantic parents sent her to Jerusalem to "rescue" him (she was unsuccessful), she ended up writing a lengthy and sympathetic article about Aish and Rav Noach Weinberg that was published in *Rolling Stone*. Months later, a Jewish college student touring Southeast Asia visited a Buddhist ashram (*nebach*) in a search for meaning, and the Buddhist Monk, a Jewish young man (double *nebach*) from New York showed the student the *Rolling Stone* article and suggested that he spend time at Aish HaTorah (I am not making this up)—and he did!

There are few better candidates for a *ben Torah*'s scorn than Jewish Buddhist monks, rock 'n roll critics, and *Rolling Stone* magazine. Yet we should view them, every person, and everything as unwitting agents carrying out Hashem's plan in ways we can or cannot see. This will elevate our view of the world all around us, and since we too have a place in the plan, it will elevate our view of ourselves.

This ends the material on which I gave shiurim more than once over the years. What follows are a few insights taken from the remaining Mishnayos that I believe are worth sharing.

ו. רבי ישמעאל בר רבי יוסי אומר הלומד על מנת ללמד מספיקין בידו ללמוד וללמד והלומד על מנת לעשות מספיקין בידו ללמוד וללמד לשמור ולעשות.

Mishnah 6. Rabbi Yishmael bar Rabbi Yosi says: One who learns in order to be able to teach, they (Heaven) grant him the means to learn and to teach. But one who learns in order to be able to do (the mitzvos), they grant him the means to learn and to teach, to keep (the negative commandments) and to do (the positive commandments).

The Mishnah teaches us several new things:

1. One who sincerely desires to study Torah will be given Heavenly assistance.
2. Learning Torah to be able to teach, even if ego driven (in the old days, teaching Torah was not a job that paid a salary), is nonetheless meritorious and worthy of Divine assistance.
3. The preferred motivation for learning Torah is in order to be able to do the mitzvos (probably the meaning of *lishmah* in Chapter 6, Mishnah 1), and it makes one worthy of much more assistance.

That being so, we have to ask: Why don't we do it? Most people who learn Gemara (outside of *Mo'ed* and *Chullin*) do not trace each halachah down to the *Shulchan Aruch*, and even among those who do, very few will then spend time learning the contemporary *poskim* (halachic decisors). Younger students focus almost exclusively on Gemara in order to learn skills, but why don't most of us learn "in order to do" later in life?

I don't know. Rav Yisrael Salanter did say that children studying *Bava Metzia* learn that other people's property rights must be respected, which is a form of learning in order to do. But in one of his Thursday night talks, Rav Avigdor Miller said the following: "When a person learns Gemara, at first it seems to be just halachos. But the halachos enter your mind, and you become aware of the tremendous principles that every *Masechta* and every *sugya* talk about: in *kedushah* and service of Hakadosh Baruch Hu and loving His Torah…" So in all our learning, there is at least an element of this.

כג. רבי שמעון בן אלעזר אומר אל תרצה את חברך בשעת כעסו
ואל תנחמהו בשעה שמתו מוטל לפניו ואל תשאל לו בשעת נדרו
ואל תשתדל לראותו בשעת קלקלתו.

Mishnah 23. Rabbi Shimon ben Elazar says: Do not pacify your friend in the time of his anger, and do not comfort him when his dead lies before him, and do not question him at the time of his [making a] vow, and do not try to see him at the time of his disgrace.

Let's examine these four cases and then consider what their common denominator might be.

"Do not pacify your friend in the time of his anger"—Shmeryl is in a rage, furious with Beryl, or with you, or with the universe. He is in no mood right now to accept your arguments why he should forgive Beryl (or you or the universe), and once he rejects your arguments today, he is less likely to accept them even tomorrow after he has calmed down. So wait.

"Do not comfort him when his dead lies before him"—In the presence of a loved one who has just died, the mourner is in grief-stricken shock. A hug may be appropriate, but words of consolation will have no effect, and the mourner might think your words display terrible insensitivity. So wait.

"Do not question him at the time of his (making a) vow"—A *talmid chacham* can annul Shmeryl's vow if it had been made without considering its ramifications. "Had you realized, when you vowed never to speak to your son-in-law, that it might mean never seeing your grandchildren, would you have made the vow?"

"No, I would not have vowed."

"Then it is permitted (annulled)."

But if Shmeryl has just now made the vow in a fit of anger, and you ask that question, he might say, "I don't care; I would have said it regardless," and the vow will never be annulled. So wait.

"Do not try to see him at the time of his disgrace"—If Shmeryl's boss has just now publicly humiliated him, or he has just now run out of the shul *kiddush* after falling into the punch bowl, you going to see him will only add to his embarrassment. So wait.

The point of this Mishnah seems to be that, "For everything there is a time" (*Koheles* 3:1), and before saying helpful words, we should make certain it is the right time to speak. True as that is, the Mishnah may be using these examples to illustrate a larger point: In helping others, it is not enough to want to help. We must also carefully consider how our act of kindness will be received. *Chessed* is an art, and a kind heart must be accompanied by a thoughtful mind.

Appeasing, comforting, and questioning at the wrong time can be counterproductive, but some kind words are counterproductive at *any* time. If your friend was publicly humiliated, it may be best to pretend you did not hear it, and if he fell into the punch bowl, pretend you did not see it (even a week later, don't try to give comfort by telling him how you once fell into a cholent pot). If his business failed, don't tell him what he could have done if it's now too late to do, and if his father died after surgery, don't ask him why he had not first consulted Dr. So and So.

כח. רבי אלעזר הקפר אומר הקנאה והתאוה והכבוד מוציאין את האדם מן העולם.

Mishnah 28. Rabbi Elazar Hakappar says: Envy, lust, and honor remove a person from the world.

"Lust"—We should not need a Mishnah to tell us that lust for forbidden things brings ruination. The Mishnah refers to lust even for kosher pleasures.

"Honor"—Although receiving honors can be hazardous to one's spiritual health, especially if you develop a taste for it, in this Mishnah honor means *seeking* honor.

"The world" means *this* world.

For example: Shmeryl and Kreinchy, a young couple with two adorable little children, buy their first house in a nice neighborhood with a vibrant shul nearby. They are very happy, and "all's right in the world" they live in. But after a while, Kreinchy begins to notice ads in *frum* magazines (the only sort of magazines they read) for much larger houses and much fancier clothing, while Shmeryl sees ads for expensive wine and top-of-the-line steaks that they really can't afford.

The thought preys on them: To get the (perfectly kosher) things they lust after, should they go into debt via loans or credit cards? If they get caught in the money trap, it can bring their world crashing down. And even if they do the right thing and resolve to live within their means, the feeling of missing out—of being deprived of so many things they desire—gnaws at their happiness, and they no longer live in the world of contentment that was once theirs.

"Envy"—Shmeryl and Kreinchy got rid of their magazines and are no longer tempted by ads. However, they can't help noticing that their friendly neighbor's car is bigger, the neighbor's kitchen is newer, and her kids are dressed in matching designer clothes. The young couple had been happy, but by comparing themselves to the neighbors, they become less so. As feelings of envy fester, they come to resent their neighbors, as if the neighbors had done them harm, and in addition to leaving their world of contentment, they are no longer living in the world of rational thought (also known as "reality").

"Honor"—After giving up on magazines and neighbors, Shmeryl and Kreinchy throw themselves into volunteer work for their shul. At the shul's annual dinner, of which they put in many hours of work as members of the dinner committee, they are a little disappointed (or maybe more than a little disappointed) not to have been chosen as honorees. Being *frum* and at least somewhat idealistic, they have no complaints—that is, until the MC mentions by name all those who made the dinner possible, except for Shmeryl and Kreinchy.

They leave early, Kreinchy in tears, both vowing never to work for any shul or to have anything to do with "those people" again. If you ask, they would tell you, "We don't seek honor, but to be humiliated?!" In reality, there had been no humiliation, only an inadvertent oversight, and the desire for honor has shattered their world for no good reason at all.

Chapter Five

א. בעשרה מאמרות נברא העולם ומה תלמוד לומר והלא במאמר אחד יכול להבראות אלא להפרע מן הרשעים שמאבדין את העולם שנברא בעשרה מאמרות וליתן שכר טוב לצדיקים שמקיימין את העולם שנברא בעשרה מאמרות.

Mishnah 1. With ten utterances the world was created, and what does this teach us? Could it not have been created with one utterance? But it is to punish the wicked who destroy the world that was created with ten utterances, and to grant good reward to the righteous who sustain the world that was created with ten utterances.

Obviously, it was not more work for Hashem to make the world with multiple utterances; and if it is to impress upon us how vast is the world for which we are responsible, are we indeed more impressed and inspired to keep the mitzvos by the fact of ten utterances?

But perhaps (and I suggest it only as a possibility), the Mishnah is teaching us that the world is made up of many separate component parts working together, and our smallest deeds (good or otherwise) can have a huge impact in times and places far from our own.

For example:

- A butcher in Czarist Russia gave train fare to two boys to enable them to travel to learn in Slabodka Yeshiva. It was an act of great *chessed* for two boys, but he had no way of knowing that

117

in sending young Aharon Kotler and Yaakov Kamenetsky to yeshiva, he was doing a great *chessed* for all of Klal Yisrael.

- In 1754, George Washington requested a commission as an officer in the *British* army. Had his request been granted, the American Revolution might never have gotten off the ground.

- At a meeting of the newly independent thirteen colonies in 1784, a motion was made to ban slavery from all future states, which almost certainly would have prevented the Civil War that cost six hundred thousand lives. The votes in favor would have been seven to six, except that the delegate from New Jersey was absent that day, and with a six-to-six tie, the motion failed.

- When Turkey entered World War I as an ally of Germany, David Ben-Gurion requested permission to create a legion of Jewish soldiers in Eretz Yisrael to fight *on the side of the Turks.* Among other consequences, it would have meant no Balfour Declaration; fortunately, the Turks turned him down.

There is an infinite number of such examples—how a particular *shidduch* came to be is often a good one—teaching us that the world is infinitely complex, and, having an idea how our smallest act impacts the world, it behooves us (and inspires us with pride!) to take our responsibilities seriously.

ג....היו מכעיסין ובאין עד שבא אברהם אבינו וקבל שכר כלם.

Mishnah 3....[The ten generations from Noach to Avraham] continued to anger Him, until our father Avraham came and received the reward of all of them.

This Mishnah parallels the previous Mishnah ("Ten generations from Adam to Noach continued to anger Him"), but does not end as that Mishnah does, by mentioning punishment. Rabbeinu Yonah says that this is because "our father Avraham made up for all the deficiencies and did good deeds equal *(k'neged)* to all their evil, and saved them from punishment." It's probably asking too much to say that a *tzaddik* can save us all from punishment even in the Next World, but it is surely heartening to know that *tzaddikim* cause Hashem to look kindly upon the rest of us in their merit.

"Received the reward of all of them"—i.e., the more wickedness there is in the world, the more difficult it is to be righteous, and the greater the reward. Now, it is understandable that Avraham's wicked neighbors made it more difficult for him to be righteous, but did the wickedness of generations that preceded him also make it more difficult that he should receive reward because of them as well?

The answer is that wickedness has a cumulative effect on the world (so does righteousness!), and the deeds of long-dead sinners add to the difficulty of living virtuously. This, of course, means that today, after decades and decades of moral collapse, every mitzvah we do is worth that much more, and we should consider the possibility that Hashem holds us in higher esteem than we do ourselves.

ד. עשרה נסיונות נתנסה אברהם אבינו ועמד בכלם להודיע כמה חבתו של אברהם אבינו.

Mishnah 4. With ten trials [nisyonos] our father Avraham was tested, and he withstood them all, to make known how beloved our father Avraham is.

The Mishnah is coming to answer the famous question: Since Hashem knows the future, he knows what Avraham will do, so what need is there for the trial? One answer is that a person becomes greater when his moral courage is put into action. The word *"nisayon"* is from the word *"nes,"* a banner raised high, and "G-d tested (*nisah*) Abraham" means that He gave Avraham opportunity for elevation.

Our Mishnah gives a different answer: The trial was not for Avraham, but for *us*. The Midrash tells us: "A man is obligated to say, 'When will my deeds be like the deeds of our Patriarchs?'" We are to reach for the stars; even if we fall far short, it will at least raise us out of the mud. With this approach, "G-d tested Abraham" means that He raised him high to be a banner of inspiration for all generations. *"Atah yadati*—Now I know that you fear G-d," can be read, "*Atah yidati*—Now I have made known" to the world.

———————————————

ט. שבעה דברים בגולם ושבעה בחכם. חכם אינו מדבר לפני מי
שגדול ממנו בחכמה ובמנין ואינו נכנס לתוך דברי חברו ואינו
נבהל להשיב...ומודה על האמת. וחלופיהן בגולם.

Mishnah 9. There are seven characteristics of a golem and seven of a wise person. A wise person does not speak before [i.e., in the presence of] one who is greater in wisdom or years; he does not interrupt the words of his friend; he is not rushed to reply...and he admits the truth. And the opposite of these in a golem.

A *golem* is a lump of clay not yet worked on to give it shape and form, and a human *golem* is a lump not yet formed into a complete human being. The Mishnah is telling us that wisdom is not merely an extra bit of achievement—like the ability to speak Latin or play the trombone—but it is a quality without which a person is not fully human. The Mishnah also seems to imply that there is no middle ground between wisdom and *golem*-ness, though perhaps possessing some but not all of the seven characteristics is an in-between state.

"He does not speak before one greater in wisdom or years"—This is more than good manners. A lover of wisdom cherishes the opportunity to learn from anyone who possesses more wisdom or more experience, and he will not speak if he has much to gain by listening.

"He does not interrupt"—He does not make the mistake of believing he knows exactly what the other person plans to say before he says it.

"He is not rushed to reply"—I thought I knew what this meant, and perhaps even fooled myself into believing I practiced it, until I had occasion to telephone Rav Elya Svei to ask his opinion on something. I posed my question, and it was followed by a long silence, until I finally asked: "Um...is the Rosh Yeshiva still there?" To which he replied, "Yes, I'm thinking about your question." And I realized that this had never happened to me before. To not feel rushed to reply and truly consider what the other person has just said before answering is rare, with many conversations being more like competing monologues. Try making a short pause before responding to the other person's question or remark. It won't in itself make you a wise man or woman, but it's a good start.

"And he admits the truth"—Doesn't this characterize a *tzaddik* rather than a wise person? But the truly wise person subordinates his ego to his love of wisdom (see Chapter 4, Mishnah 1), and his joy at discovering the truth and being able to correct the error in his thinking pushes aside considerations of ego. Once in a shiur, I taught a new halachah, and a pious but unlearned man became very upset: "You mean I've been doing it wrong all these years?" The yeshiva man in the shiur, though, was *happy* to finally get it right.

We may think that we ourselves willingly admit the truth, but there are different levels of admission. If my *chavrusa* marshals proof that his position is the correct one, which of the following is the response of a true *chacham*: (a) "I hear what you're saying"; (b) "You make a good point"; (c) "You're right"; or (d) "You're right, and I'm wrong"?

יג. ארבע מדות באדם האומר שלי שלי ושלך שלך זו מדה בינונית ויש אומרים זו מדת סדום. שלי שלך ושלך שלי עם הארץ. שלי שלך ושלך שלך חסיד. שלך שלי ושלי שלי רשע.

Mishnah 13. There are four types of character [middos] among people. One who says, "What is mine is mine, and what is yours is yours," this is the average type, but some say this is the character of Sodom. "What is mine is yours, and what is yours is mine" is an am ha'aretz [ignoramus]. "What is mine is yours, and what is yours is yours" is a chassid. "What is yours is mine, and what is mine is mine" is a wicked person.

This begins a series of "there are four types" Mishnayos: four types of temperament, four types of students, four types of donors etc. It is striking that this first Mishnah does not say "there are four types of people who relate to possessions" but simply "there are four types of character among people." This fits well with Rav Dessler's teachings in *Michtav Me'Eliyahu* that the world is made up of "givers" and "takers," and being a giver or taker is one of the most fundamental traits of character that sum up a person.

This point is even more sharply made according to the opinion that "what is mine is mine, and what is yours is yours," is the character of Sodom, meaning that there is no average in-between type, and we must choose to be either a giver/*chassid* or a citizen of Sodom.

"What is mine is yours, and what is yours is mine" does not refer to actions (because if I take what is yours, I am a thief, not an *am ha'aretz*) but to *attitudes*. "We're all *heimish* here in the yeshiva, and I don't mind if you take what I leave in the fridge, so you won't mind if I take yours, right?" If he consents to my taking his food only because he is embarrassed to refuse, I am a thief. But even with his sincere consent, my attitude that I should be able to make free with his possessions (since I allow him the same freedom with mine) is that of *am ha'aretz*. When the Torah uses the word "*yekum*" (*Devarim* 11), Chazal explain that it means "a person's material possessions (*mamono*) that stand (*yakum*) him up on his feet (*Sanhedrin* 110). A *chassid* is happy to share what he has with an open hand, but it is indeed his. And someone who does not want to share with others but happily takes whatever others will share with him has the *middah* of a *rasha*, even if he doesn't violate any halachah at all.

כ. כל מחלוקת שהיא לשם שמים סופה להתקיים...זו מחלוקת
הלל ושמאי...

Mishnah 20. Any dispute that is for the sake of Heaven will endure [ArtScroll translates "will have a constructive outcome"]...the dispute between Hillel and Shammai...

Both Hillel and Shammai understood that the other's motivation was "for the sake of Heaven," and each side acknowledged that the other was following a Torah path, even when they differed as to conclusions. But what about the famous controversy over the *Rambam*'s writings, or the Vilna Gaon against Chassidim, where at least one side believed the other was *not* following the Torah and was even going *against* the Torah?

What we understand from our *rebbeim* is that here too, since later generations judged both sides to have acted for the sake of Heaven, their disputes all had a constructive outcome.

For centuries, the *Rambam*'s philosophical writings have enlightened and deepened the understanding of thousands of students, and the *Rambam*'s opponents have given those same students a necessary layer of caution—that they should not give philosophy more than its due and leave the path of Torah and *emunah* (faith). Chassidic teachings and practices inspire even many students in non-Chassidic yeshivas, and opposition forced Chassidim to develop yeshivas to demonstrate that they too could produce serious *lomdei Torah*.

Elsewhere (*In Search of Torah Wisdom*, Mosaica Press 2012, pp. 35–41), I have written about twentieth-century and contemporary Orthodox disputes—how they too have in many cases had a constructive outcome, with both sides contributing to service of Hashem. But not wishing to create yet another dispute, I'll end my discussion of this subject here.

כג–כד. יהודה בן תימא אומר הוי עז כנמר וקל כנשר רץ כצבי
וגבור כארי לעשות רצון אביך שבשמים. הוא היה אומר עז פנים
לגיהנם ובושת פנים לגן עדן. יהי רצון מלפניך ה' אלקינו ואלקי
אבותינו שיבנה בית המקדש במהרה בימינו ותן חלקנו בתורתך.

Mishnah 23–24. Yehudah ben Teima says: Be bold [az] as a leopard, light as an eagle, swift as a deer, and strong as a lion to do the will of your Father Who is in Heaven. He used to say: The brazen [az panim] goes to Gehinnom, and the shamefaced to the Garden of Eden. May it be Your Will...that the Holy Temple be built speedily in our days, and give us our share in your Torah.

The concluding sentence is familiar from the end of *Shemoneh Esreh*, but what is its connection to the rest of the Mishnah? One explanation

I saw is that every *middah* (character trait) can be used in serving Hashem, but certain *middos* (e.g., cruelty toward the wicked) if used too often become ingrained and end up being used in the wrong way. *Azus* (boldness, brazenness, disregard for what others might say or think) is necessary to be able to persist in doing the right thing in the face of ridicule, but if it becomes a habit, then "the brazen goes to *Gehinnom*." We therefore pray for the coming of Mashiach when we will no longer have to use this *middah* to fight for Hashem.

But if this is the Mishnah's meaning, shouldn't it have said, "May it be Your Will to bring Mashiach, or the final redemption"? Why focus on the Holy Temple? And (a question we can also ask about its meaning in *Shemoneh Esreh*), why do we not have our share in the Torah without the Temple? If it means we are missing out on all the mitzvos performed in the Temple, as of course we are, would we ever refer to these mitzvos as "our share (or portion) in Your Torah"?

Perhaps the meaning is: When we meet certain outstanding *tzaddikim*, we can sense that we are in the presence of an elevated spiritual personality. But why do we not see this in every *ben Torah* who learns and davens and does mitzvos all the time? One answer is that mitzvos for the soul are analogous to nutrition for the body. A diet rich in protein but missing iron or vitamin C is better than a diet missing all three, but without the necessary vitamins, you will not see in this person's face the shine of robust health.

In the same way, every mitzvah is nutrition for the soul, but only with all the mitzvos together (including those of the Temple) does the soul have the nutrition to shine in this life. Thus we ask for the Holy Temple when all our mitzvos together will create *our* share in Torah, manifesting in us our individual unique spirituality, and of course obviating the need for *middos* like *azus*.

כו. בן הא הא אומר לפום צערא אגרא.

Mishnah 26. Ben Hei says: According to the pain or suffering [tzaar] is the reward.

"According to the *tzaar* is the reward"—ArtScroll translates *tzaar* as "exertion," so the Mishnah is saying: In the case of two yeshiva students, with Chaim having a high IQ and a phenomenal memory and David not being so gifted but working harder, then even though Chaim accomplishes much more, David will receive the greater reward. But don't we know this already? What new idea is the Mishnah coming to teach us?

Here are three answers:

1. Before we learned this Mishnah, is it true that we "already know" that according to the exertion is the reward? It does not say so anywhere in *Chumash*. But the main source of our knowledge is this Mishnah itself (though similar ideas are found in the Gemara and Midrashim), and Ben Hei Hei's teaching has become so well-known that we neglect to give him credit for it. (Review the anecdote about Rav Isser Zalman Meltzer in the first Mishnah of Chapter 2.)

2. In another case of three yeshiva students who are all highly intelligent, Reuven has a natural taste for Gemara and is a hard worker to boot, while Shimon learns Gemara but does not enjoy it, and Levi finds Gemara difficult because he is by nature somewhat lazy: If "according to the exertion is the reward," then Reuven will receive far more reward because he works much harder. But if *tzaar* means pain or suffering, then Shimon and Levi (who find Gemara study positively painful) will receive enormous reward for any studying they manage to do. Many struggling yeshiva students are unaware of this point, and it is a mitzvah to let them know of it.

3. Instead of asking why the Mishnah tells us what we already know, we could ask: Is it indeed true that reward is according to *tzaar*? In Chapter 2, Mishnah 21, when Rabbi Tarfon says, "If you have studied much Torah, they will give you much reward," doesn't he imply that gifted Chaim (above) is given more reward than hard-working David who put in the hours but was unable to learn as much?

The two Mishnayos might not contradict one another. More Torah study means more reward, and the amount of reward for each moment of study varies according to the level of *tzaar*. But even so, consider two yeshiva students, Nachman and Shea, who are both sincere and hard-working, but Nachman has a much better head. Nachman ends up becoming a famous Rosh Yeshiva, while Shea ends up as the cook in Nachman's yeshiva. Do we really believe that in the next world, Shea's reward will equal Nachman's, or even be superior, if he put in a bit more effort than his hard-working friend?

I don't claim to understand, but for an idea I heard from Rav Avigdor Miller—and I pray that I heard correctly—see Chapter 2, Mishnah 21, and a possible explanation there.

Chapter Six

ב. והמכתב מכתב אלקים הוא חרות על הלוחות. אל תקרי חרות
אלא חרות שאין לך בן חורין אלא מי שעוסק בתלמוד תורה.

*Mishnah 2....And the writing was the writing of G-d engraved
[charus] on the Tablets. Do not read it charus rather cheirus,
for you have no ben chorin except one who is engaged in the
study of Torah.*

*C*heirus is translated as "freedom," a *ben chorin* is "a free man,"
and the Mishnah is saying that only the person engaged
in Torah study has true freedom. What does this mean? In
Midrash Rabbah, Rabbi Nechemyah says that the verse means "free from
the Angel of Death," but we do not see how this is so. I believe the most
common interpretation is "freedom from the *yetzer hara*." Immersed
in Torah study, a man's soul is connected to holiness, and his mind is
occupied so that there is no room for sinful thoughts.

But perhaps another approach is to ask: Does *ben chorin* really mean
"free man"? The term appears only once in Tanach: "Woe to you, land,
whose king is a lad (acc. to *Rashi*, acts like an adolescent)...Happy are
you, land, whose king is a *ben chorin*" (*Koheles* 10:16–17). In that verse,
ben chorin here seems to be the opposite of "acting like an adolescent,"
i.e., a man of maturity. There, ArtScroll translates *ben chorin* as "a man
of dignity," and *Ibn Ezra* explains *ben chorin* as "*she'yaaseh maaseh
ha'gedolim*—he acts in the manner of great men."

127

If that is also the meaning of the term in our Mishnah, it is saying: Only one who engages in Torah study lives a life of true dignity and greatness. Even a king or prime minister engaged in the affairs of the state spends most of his day thinking about his personal needs and desires, and even in his work for the good of the country, he must spend a lot of time on petty matters like public appearances, ceremonies, persuading, cajoling, threatening, and manipulating. But the diligent Torah student spends his day and much of the night in the greatness of Hashem's Torah—holiness that elevates him above the petty and the transitory.

This also fits well with connecting *cheirus* with *charus* (engraving). Engraving has nothing to do with freedom, in which case the *derashah* is derived only from the identical letters. But if a *ben chorin* is someone of dignity and importance, engraving too is used to record words that are of great and lasting importance, like the Tablets, and the *derashah* is derived from a similarity of concept as well as letters.

———

ו....התורה נקנית בארבעים ושמונה דברים...במעוט תענוג...השמח
בחלקו...נושא בעול עם חברו...והאומר דבר בשם אומרו...

Mishnah 6....The Torah is acquired [niknes] by means of forty-eight qualifications:...limited pleasure...being happy with one's portion...sharing the yoke with his friend...saying a thing in the name of the one who said it...

Rav Aharon Kotler pointed out that the word *niknes* (acquired) is like the word *kinyan* (method of acquisition). Even if a buyer and a seller agree to a transaction at a certain price, transfer of ownership does not occur until a legal act of *kinyan* takes place. For instance, a buyer giving money or a seller giving a document of sale is an effective *kinyan* for real estate, but not for movable objects, whose *kinyan* is made by the buyer lifting the object. Rav Aharon therefore concluded that if the Mishnah tells us that Torah requires these forty-eight *kinyanim*, a seeker after Torah *must* use these, and no other *kinyanim* will suffice.

It is a well-known tradition that when our ancestors left Egypt, the forty-nine days leading up to the first Shavuos were a time of preparing to receive the Torah, and every year we should use this same time to prepare to personally receive the Torah ourselves. On each of the first forty-eight days of counting the *omer*, we should contemplate and try to strengthen within ourselves one of these forty-eight *kinyanim*. On day forty-nine, we should review them all and try to integrate them all into one harmonious whole to become a person worthy of acquiring Hashem's Torah.

MANY OF THESE QUALIFICATIONS (attentive listening, closeness with colleagues, asking and answering, etc.) are also important in order to acquire expertise in secular disciplines, but "limited pleasure" and "saying a thing in the name of the one who said it" are not prerequisites for becoming a philosopher or a mathematician. But as we say in our daily *birchos haTorah*, it is Hashem Who teaches us Torah, even today, and a degree of virtue, holiness, and distancing from material pleasures is necessary to merit that Divine assistance.

Most of today's Torah teachers no longer speak about abstaining from our abundance of kosher physical pleasures. Perhaps they think it too much to ask of our generation, or perhaps they have decided that with so many non-kosher temptations facing young people today, we should not make an issue of indulging in kosher ones. But we should at least know such an idea exists: In Brooklyn's Yeshivas Bais Hatalmud in the 1950s, someone installed a water cooler. When one of the Roshei Yeshiva saw it, he demanded that it be removed, saying: "The yeshiva is not a park!"

"Being happy with one's portion"—A serious Torah student must surely be satisfied with his lot in material things so as not to spend excessive time and energy pursuing money. But even in spiritual things, we need a delicate balance: to always want to learn more, while at the same time savoring what we've already achieved. A student who finishes a *masechta* might think: "What's the big deal of learning one *masechta*? I'll never finish *Shas*, so why continue?" Rav Shlomo Freifeld gave an award to a *baal teshuvah* who completed the study of a single page of Gemara (!), and we too should use every page as an opportunity to give ourselves both a pat on the back (for what we've accomplished) and a kick in the pants (to do even more).

"SHARING THE YOKE WITH HIS FRIEND"—This is the quality of *empathy*, a word so commonly misused that we have to clarify its true meaning. "Sympathy" means to feel *for* the other person, while "empathy" means to feel *what* the other person is feeling. If Reuven's father has just died, *r"l*, his friend Shimon who has never suffered a loss, can express sympathy ("I'm sorry for your loss"), but only if he too had lost a parent can he express empathy ("I feel your pain"). "Sharing the yoke" means to try as best we can to develop empathy by imagining ourselves in the other person's place, even if we have never been there.

This applies to happy occasions, too. If your friend is getting married or has become a new father, try to imagine his joy and do your best to feel it too (if you can't attend a friend's wedding, you might still drink a *l'chaim* and sing a little that day).

Empathy is a beautiful quality, but what does it have to do with acquiring Torah? Rav Simcha Zissel Ziv explained: Torah development means learning to comprehend that which we do not yet comprehend—not only additional facts but new perspectives, which require us to step outside ourselves to see the subject from a different point of view. "Why did *Tosafos* not explain the Gemara as I would have? How would *Rashi* respond to *Tosafos'* argument? Why would *Tosafos* not be satisfied with that response?" etc. We must seek to rise above our limitations to try to climb on the shoulders of giants to dimly perceive what they so clearly saw.

ט. אמר רבי יוסי בן קסמא פעם אחת הייתי מהלך בדרך ופגע בי
אדם אחד ונתן לי שלום והחזרתי לו שלום. אמר לי רבי מאיזה
מקום אתה. אמרתי לו מעיר גדולה של חכמים ושל סופרים
אני. אמר לי רבי רצונך שתדור עמנו במקומנו ואני אתן לך אלף
אלפים דנרי זהב ואבנים טובות ומרגליות אמרתי לו אם אתה
נותן לי כל כסף וזהב ואבנים טובות ומרגליות שבעולם אין אני
דר אלא במקום תורה...

Mishnah 9. Rabbi Yosi ben Kisma said: I was once traveling on the road, and a man met me...He said, "Rebbi, would you be willing to live with us in our place? I will give you a thousand thousands of gold dinars and precious stones and pearls." I said to him: "If you would give me all the silver and gold and precious stones and pearls in the world, I would not live anywhere except in a place of Torah..."

In the yeshivos, they ask, half in jest: "Why didn't Rabbi Yosi take all the silver and gold and establish a *kollel* in that town, transforming it into a place of Torah?" They answer that, regardless of funding, some communities are simply not suited to becoming places of Torah.

There seems to be some truth to this. The Gemara says that while Ezra became a great Torah teacher in Bavel, Daniel and Mordechai, who lived in the province of Eilam, were unable to develop a large body of students. In Eastern Europe, almost all the great yeshivas were in small towns, not in Vilna, Kovno, or Minsk. And it is said that Rav Aharon Kotler deliberately chose to establish his yeshiva in the small town of Lakewood instead of a larger community.

One reason for this might be that small towns have fewer distractions; Daniel and Mordechai lived in the capitol. It is also possible that the small towns' lower standards of living and simpler lifestyles are more conducive to Torah learning (with their "limited pleasures," as in Mishnah 6). If this is true, it would well explain Rabbi Yosi ben Kisma's refusal to move; the fabulous wealth of the new community would itself be an impediment to making it a place of Torah!

יא. כל מה שברא הקדוש ברוך הוא בעולמו לא בראו אלא לכבודו שנאמר כל הנקרא בשמי ולכבודי בראתיו יצרתיו אף עשיתיו.

Mishnah 11. All that the Holy One, blessed be He, created in His world, He created only for His glory, as it is said: "All that is called by My Name, it is for My glory that I created it; I formed it, I made it."

Why is it important for the Mishnah to teach us this?

Hashem, of course, has no need for glory or honor, but for us to achieve our purpose on earth, in addition to working at meticulous mitzvah observance, "*tzaddik be'emunaso yichyeh*," we must also develop some sort of awareness of the presence of the *Borei Olam*. (Unfortunately, some *frum* people do not know about this.) The Mishnah is teaching that an essential part of this awareness is for us to work to perceive that "*melo chol ha'aretz kevodo*—His Glory fills the world." It is so essential that we are expected to say this (and presumably think about it!) four times every day—three times in *Shacharis* and once in *Minchah*—and more on Shabbos.

So when you are outdoors and the sun is shining, birds are singing, grass is on the ground, and leaves are on the trees, marvel at the beauty and whisper: "His glory fills the world!" Try it at least once, if not constantly. When you walk into shul for davening, remind yourself that we are assembling *as a group* to proclaim to the whole world the existence of our Creator and our King (*Ramban, Parashas Bo*).

When you eat breakfast, at least once think to yourself: "I'm eating because I like to eat. But it's also true that I need to eat in order to have life and strength to do Hashem's will, so this breakfast is also a way of honoring Hashem." (See Chapter 2, Mishnah 17.)

And when you see (and worry about) how the world is going downhill so speedily that it seems unnatural, remind yourself that it *is* unnatural; it is Hashem carrying out His plan before our eyes (and we need not worry quite so much).

And if we can think about these things, even a little—if we can go outdoors and feel ourselves surrounded by Hashem's world and its beauty, basking in glory, is that not a most glorious way to live?

About the Author

AN ALUMNUS of Lakewood's Beth Medrash Govoha, Rabbi Yisroel Miller served thirty-four years in the rabbinate before his retirement in 2019. He is the author of six books.

MOSAICA PRESS

BOOK PUBLISHERS

Elegant, Meaningful & Bold

info@MosaicaPress.com
www.MosaicaPress.com

The Mosaica Press team of
acclaimed editors and designers
is attracting some of the most
compelling thinkers and teachers
in the Jewish community today.
Our books are available around
the world.

HARAV YAACOV HABER
RABBI DORON KORNBLUTH